Praise for This Book:

"The Top Ten Myths of Selling, the extensive checklists, and the worksheets are worth the price of this book alone. But what might have a bigger impact on your selling success after reading Lambert's work is the understanding, then application of the idea that great sales professionals 'Embrace a Sales Mindset' (Step 1). This just isn't taught in training, and you'd be wise to put it into play—and then see what a difference it makes in your performance."

Dan Seidman
Author and sales training consultant, SalesAutopsy.com

"Once again, Brian has written a book that will raise the bar for sales professionals around the world. This book should be required reading for all salespeople. Brian represents the next generation of thought leaders in the sales profession and following the 10 steps he outlined in this book will deliver the sales results you're looking for!"

Tony Cross
Founder, Growth Matters, South Africa

"This is a fabulous sales book that sets itself apart from the other overly simplistic approaches to selling. Take action on its contents, and you'll build long-lasting relationships and accelerate your revenue performance! It should be required reading for new and experienced sales reps alike."

Aaron Steeves
Branch Manager, Ricoh Business Solutions

"Core essentials every new rep should know and a great refresher for seasoned pros!"

Marc Ramos
Director, Sales College, Red Hat University

"This is a great book for sales managers that need to move their team from transactional to solution selling—even in the retail environment!"

Marc Imhoff
Retail Channel Senior Manager, France Telecom-Orange

"A great read. It clearly defines how you can move from salesperson to sales professional while becoming a trusted advisor to clients!"

Kevin Casper
Sales Professional, EMC

"I've been selling long enough to know a good sales book when I see one—and this is a great book. It contains everything I wish I was told but had to figure out on my own. Managers should give it to every new salesperson on the team and use it as a topic to train at sales meetings!"

Rick Tancreto
15+ years of experience selling for Fortune 500 companies

"This is a great book for any salesperson who needs to be consultative in their approach. It defines what you really need to know and do to be successful!"

Eric Kerkhoff
Account Manager, Hewlett-Packard Company

"Selling isn't easy, and learning how to leverage people, technology, processes, and conversations to move the sale forward is a must. This book helps you do that with easy checklists and words of wisdom from seasoned sales pros in an easy-to-read format."

Scott Barghaan
Client Solutions Director, Large Global IT Company

"Professional selling is complex and no one understands it better, while relating it simply, than Brian Lambert. This single book covers everything selling has become, not what it used to be. You MUST know this stuff if you want to do more than just keep up."

Tim Ohai
Strategist and Coach, Growth & Associates
Co-author of *World-Class Selling: New Sales Competencies*

"After 20 years in professional services, I found myself in a sales role. This book helped me make the transition quickly and easily."

Allan Mills, MPM, PMP
Regional Director, Eastern US Branch, True Solutions Inc.

10 STEPS TO

Successful Sales

10 STEPS TO SUCCESS

Let's face it, most people spend their days in chaotic, fast-paced, time- and resource-strained organizations. Finding time for just one more project, assignment, or even learning opportunity—no matter how career enhancing or useful—is difficult to imagine. The *10 Steps* series is designed for today's busy professional who needs advice and guidance on a wide array of topics ranging from project management to people management, from business strategy to decision making and time management, from leading effective meetings to researching and creating a compelling presentation. Each book in this new ASTD series promises to take its readers on a journey to solid understanding, with practical application the ultimate destination. This is truly a just-tell-me-what-to-do-now series. You will find action-driven language teamed with examples, worksheets, case studies, and tools to help you quickly implement the right steps and chart a path to your own success. The *10 Steps* series will appeal to a broad business audience from middle managers to upper-level management. Workplace learning and human resource professionals along with other professionals seeking to improve their value proposition in their organizations will find these books a great resource.

10 STEPS TO

Successful Sales

Brian Lambert

ASTD PRESS
Alexandria, Virginia

16 15 14 13 12 11 10 1 2 3 4 5 6 7 8 9 10

ASTD Press is an internationally renowned source of insightful and practical information on workplace learning and performance topics, including training basics, evaluation and return on investment, instructional systems development, e-learning, leadership, and career development. Visit us at www.astd.org/astdpress.

Ordering information: Books published by ASTD Press can be purchased by visiting our website at store.astd.org or by calling 800.628.2783 or 703.683.8100.

Library of Congress Control Number: 2009922422
ISBN-10: 1-56286-686-9
ISBN-13: 978-1-56286-686-0

ASTD Press Editorial Staff:
Director of Content: Dean Smith
Manager, ASTD Press: Jacqueline Edlund-Braun
Senior Associate Editor: Tora Estep
Senior Associate Editor: Justin Brusino
Editorial Assistant: Victoria DeVaux

Editorial, Design, and Production: Abella Publishing Services, LLC
Cover Design: Ana Ilieva Foreman

Printed by Versa Press, Inc., East Peoria, IL, www.versapress.com

CONTENTS

PREFACE

Nothing happens in the business world without selling something. If you've been selling for longer than a few months, you probably have realized that selling is extremely complex and involves lifelong learning and experimentation to find those strategies and tactics that increase the chances of a sale and position you to become a trusted advisor to your clients.

This book is specifically designed to help you succeed in the foundational, business-critical profession of selling. These trends are a small sample of the change (and some would say chaos) that you'll have to harness and leverage to be successful. Just like any other professional, overreliance on a specific routine or approach could be detrimental in this fast-paced environment. The market is fluid and buyers require speed and agility. *10 Steps to Successful Sales* will help you transition quickly and effectively from salesperson to sales professional while improving and reinventing yourself and your approach.

Why Another Sales Book? Most books on professional selling are considerably different than this one. When writing it, I sought to fill a void and address what I consider a crucial problem in the sales profession: a major lack of structure, framework, and definition of *what* professional selling entails. There are a lot of books on *how* to sell but few that explain what to expect. This lack of clarity creates inconsistent performance in most salespeople and stems from several factors. First, academia has yet to be recognized for advancing the sales profession. Despite the fact that there are many schools offering minors in professional selling, the academic community is not considered the catalyst that drives the sales profession forward.

Second, there hasn't been a major advance in the sales process (for example, the sales funnel) in almost 100 years. In reality, the fundamental steps of the sales process haven't changed, but many organizations and individuals have reinvented them over time (hint: memorizing a five-step process isn't going to solve all your challenges; there's more to it than that).

> At the turn of the century, there were three associations in selling and three major publications devoted to it. There were also degrees in salesmanship and there was even a global congress on selling. Since that time, the sales occupation has yet to collectively pull together into a unified profession.

Third, most salespeople have existed in a fragmented occupation without guidelines or unity. Lacking this unity, people are reinventing the wheel. Instead of 50 years of knowledge being built, we have had four years of knowledge being built (and rebuilt) over and over again. Most authors are writing and rewriting the same content, such as how to handle objections, how to ask questions, and how to close a sale. I have books in my office right now from 1912 and 1947 that talk about these same steps of the sales process. This is helpful and means there is a specific set of knowledge you need to know as a salesperson. It also means you have a choice to make: follow in the footsteps of those before you or chart your own path for sales professionalism. If you choose the latter, you can set yourself apart by gathering and internalizing sales knowledge as fast as possible to move to the higher end professional knowledge and skill you will need to be successful.

Think about it, if you were a new doctor, which would you rather have early on?

- someone telling you how to take out an appendix, how to set a broken bone, or how to take someone's blood pressure, or
- in-depth knowledge of the human body, the systems of the body, and an understanding of definitions and terminology, so you can think on your feet, make better decisions, and create new and improved methods for helping people?

A lot of what has been missing in professional selling has to do with the lack of a body of knowledge—in effect, the equivalent of *Gray's Anatomy* for the world of selling. In other words, many salespeople don't read books that will help them make the transition to trusted advisor and sales professional. Many salespeople haven't read books that define what selling is and provide a framework and structure for all the literature, tapes, and seminar content they will encounter. While this book doesn't go quite that far, you may notice that selling is more complicated than you thought—or, worse yet, than your organization believes.

10 Steps to Successful Sales is different from other sales books in other ways as well:

- This book tackles the task of explaining what selling is, providing both a broad definition and framework for the profession as well as a no-holds-barred realistic overview of what people entering the profession can expect, what they need to prepare for, and what others are likely to be doing.
- It is longer than most sales texts because I've attempted to define what selling entails in the broadest sense to establish a framework.
- It contains very little on *how* to sell. Except for Steps 5 and 7, most of this book presents information that isn't taught in most colleges or universities and isn't addressed in most sales training courses.
- It is not written in a style designed to be cute, flippant, or attention grabbing. I don't believe many of the perceptions floating around the business community—that salespeople

can't sit still for long periods of time, salespeople can't stay focused on one topic for a long time, or salespeople require a book that is chock full of pictures, jokes, or cartoons in order to get the point—I just don't believe it.

- Each chapter is written to be able to stand on its own, making *10 Steps* a great desk reference, dialogue starter, or textbook for a college class.

I have organized *10 Steps to Successful Sales* around helping you to become an effective and efficient trusted advisor. The content is derived from my own personal experiences as a top-performing, award-winning sales professional, as well as my doctoral research, interviews with hundreds of salespeople and managers, and my experiences training thousands of salespeople across the globe. More important, I don't want you to just take my word for it. I have also included the sage advice of nearly 100 "gurus" who have worked hard to personally evolve from salesperson to sales professional. They have graciously offered their words of wisdom to help you learn how to become a sales professional.

10 Steps to Successful Sales is part of the ASTD Press *10 Step* series and was written to provide you with a proven process, quick reference checklists, and tips to succeed in the sales profession regardless of the product or services in your portfolio. I hope the tips and tools contained in this book will guide you each step of the way in prospecting, presenting, following, and developing long-lasting relationships. More important, I hope this book helps you make the transition from salesperson to sales professional.

◆ ◆ ◆

I would like to thank the "gurus" who contributed their quotes to help bring this book to life. I hope their words will inspire you to work hard and evolve from salesperson to sales professional. I would like to thank the team at ASTD Press for their professionalism and support in writing this book, as well as Lynn Sparapany Lewis, for her thoughtful advice, helpful critique, and valuable copy review and editing. Special thanks to Gerhard Gschwandtner of *Selling Power* magazine and Dave Stein of ESResearch Group, for being mentors and true supporters of sales professionalism. A heartfelt "thank you" to Eric Kerkhoff and Tim Ohai, for helping me find the best way to articulate the principles and universal truths that cut across all sales situations and all vertical markets, representing all types of selling strategies. And thanks to my loving family, for supporting me in my lifelong quest to advance the sales profession.

I hope you enjoy learning what you need to know and what you need to do to be an effective and efficient trusted business advisor through the *10 Steps to Successful Sales*.

To Your Success!

Brian Lambert, PhD
Author, Trainer, and Sales Professional

INTRODUCTION

The business world today, and more specifically the marketing and selling worlds, can be summed up in one word—change. As organizations fight to grow profits, maximize shareholder value, and align internal marketing and selling processes to customer needs, the role of today's sales professional is undergoing a major transformation. This transformation is happening because sales professionals must cope with changing expectations, constantly evolving products and services, and an increased responsibility to drive top-line revenue results. At the same time, new and experienced sales professionals alike are facing tough challenges when it comes to building their careers, advancing their professional standing, or rising above the competition. That's where this book comes in: A redefined formula for salesperson success and professional advancement has now emerged.

Here's the reality. The formula for success in selling today cannot be boiled down into simplistic clichés. Success in selling requires delivery of value—that's it. But, obviously this is easier said than done. From the management of your own organization to building personal relationships on a foundation of trust, you must be able to achieve results quickly while bringing relevant skills to fray so you can begin making an impact quickly.

The Real First Step

While this book has taken a 10-step approach to sales success that begins with embracing a sales mindset on page 3, you will get even greater value by reading and working through the two appendices located in the back of the book. *Introduction to the World of Selling,* Appendix A, sets the context for selling in today's changing environment. You will find a brief, valuable history of the profession and what is different about selling today, as well as new customer and CEO expectations. Start here if you are curious about learning from those who have come before you.

Appendix B, *Top Ten Myths of Selling*, offers both stereotype-busting advice and solid tips that will help you apply the 10 steps to become a successful sales professional. Start here if you're not quite sure of what you're getting into. The myths may surprise you!

These appendix chapters will be noted, and in some cases referenced, as you read the book, but I recommend you spend a little time with this valuable material before diving into the book.

Success in selling requires a fine balance. It requires a balance between art and science—between skill and intuition. To get it right, you have to engage in a process of self-discovery, self-awareness, and professional exploration—and this book will help you begin the process of continuous improvement.

Professional selling is not as simple as completing the transfer of products or services to a buyer. There are decisions to be made, conversations to have, and knowledge to gain. On one hand, there are individual buying decisions; on the other hand, there are organizational processes. The science involves following sound sales processes—that is, identifying and following the tactical and strategic processes that increase the probability of selling a product or service to a person or group of people. Sales processes are composed of methodologies or approaches that increase the chance of closing a sale. As part of this process, you must determine who the target buyers are, assess client needs, and determine which products or services will help your client capitalize on a business opportunity or solve a specific problem. But processes are embedded within the system required to sell, and this system is composed of strategies, tools, and innovation. That's why this book offers much more than other books—you'll learn about the systems approach necessary for success from the very beginning, so you can build momentum, increase sales velocity, and increase your capacity to sell.

Just remember, an overreliance on many of today's published sales processes and sales funnels can be detrimental. It's just not as simple as following a nicely packaged, rote process funnel. While the sales processes and funnels may look great on paper, it's just one tool you need to be successful. You have to be a creative and strategic thinker who is able to harness knowledge, make plans, organize workflow, and set priorities. In other words, you must learn to use the complexity around you. A sales process can help, but it's just a start.

The art of selling requires you to achieve the level of trusted advisor—a competent sales professional with the expertise to clearly articulate product and service benefits while effectively educating the buyer so he or she can make a well-informed decision. This requires listening and communication skills, negotiation, energy, enthusiasm, ambition, relationship building, honesty, integrity, ethics, credibility, initiative, self-awareness, adaptability, and—most important—trust.

This book, *10 Steps to Successful Sales*, provides a framework you can use to understand the art and science of selling. It will help you understand two often overlooked questions for new salespeople: *"What do I need to know?"* and *"What do I need to do?"* Remember these two questions because they exemplify the competencies of most successful sales professionals, and they help you build critical momentum in any job that involves persuasion and influence.

As you begin exploring the complexities of selling, it is easy to get caught up in the complexity around you. No matter what your experience level or where you are in your career, in these pages you will find proven techniques and tips to help you succeed in becoming a sales professional.

In particular, you will learn how to

- develop the right sales mindset and assess your strengths and weaknesses
- explain the five buckets of key information that all sales professionals need to know
- identify the five reasons why people buy
- share the habits of successful salespeople
- describe five levels of effectiveness known as the "Universal Sales Truths"
- demystify the myths of selling
- determine where you are with prospects and clients in the sales process
- provide strategies to sharpen verbal and nonverbal communication skills, including listening skills and questioning techniques
- define the seven roles of highly competent sales professionals
- effectively set and manage expectations with internal teams and external clients.

Structure of This Book

No matter what industry you serve or job title you hold, you will find that each section describes one of the 10 specific steps necessary for accomplishing the goal of moving you from sales "person" to sales "professional." To get there, you need to embrace an approach that helps you become an effective and efficient trusted advisor. For that reason, this book is divided into three main sections that focus on

- **Effectiveness**—defined as something that is adequate to accomplish a purpose or something that produces the intended or expected result. Simply put, sales effectiveness is about accomplishing set goals. You'll learn this valuable skill in this section.

- **Efficiency**—defined as competency in performance. Sales efficiency is about getting things done and can be improved by meeting the buyer where they are at, following a standard sales process, and creating your own personal sales system. You'll learn the keys to efficiency in this section.
- **Becoming a trusted advisor**—a trusted advisor is someone who is customer focused and is therefore respected and trusted by clients and customers. You'll learn how to take what you've learned and apply it in this section.

The book is also divided into chapters by the key step they discuss and illuminate. As discussed earlier, the appendixes, along with the free bonus materials located at www.10stepstosales.com/bonuses, also play an important part in ensuring your transformation into a successful selling professional. And you may wish to start there.

Section 1: How to Be Effective

- **Step 1: Embrace a Sales Mindset.** Selling is not simply about encouraging a customer to buy a product or service. It is also about listening, analyzing, problem solving, and persuading. Selling is conversation and communication in order to become a trusted advisor. This chapter focuses on striving for accountability, objectively determining your strengths and weaknesses, understanding your personal selling style, relating actions to personal outputs, and mastering the Continuous Selling Improvement Cycle, as well as highlights the importance of understanding your role in relation to the buyer and how to become a more competent sales professional by optimizing your strengths.
- **Step 2: Know Your Job and Your Role.** When starting any new job, it is important to understand exactly what is expected so that you can meet or exceed the expectations. Oftentimes, these expectations are not explicit and are nearly impossible to achieve because measures and

benchmarks are vague or nonexistent. This chapter focuses on the four key benefits of the sales profession, how organizations define sales strategies and market segmentation, and the seven functions of any sales job.

- **Step 3: Develop Winning Habits.** Every successful sales professional has mastered habits—most of which were learned on the job. Small and consistent changes in your activities can have a significant impact on productivity. This chapter focuses on examining the activities that add value and increase productivity so you can determine how to appropriately allocate your time. In particular, this chapter delves into defining your quota, building a pipeline, determining your priorities, and executing your plan of action.

Section 2: How to Be Efficient

- **Step 4: Understand the Buying Process.** Understanding how clients buy services or products can make or break your sales pipeline. It isn't enough to know how to market and sell; you have to understand how your clients buy. This chapter reviews the buying process, how customers define value, who influences the buying decisions in an organization, and negotiating strategies for closing the deal.
- **Step 5: Leverage the Sales Process.** Understanding the *buying* process is only half of the equation; understanding the *selling* process is equally important because it enables you to customize to meet your own personal needs. This chapter details a seven-part sales process, describes the outputs, and provides strategies to help you master each part of the process.
- **Step 6: Create Your Own Personal Selling System.** To maximize efficiency and make your own success, you need to use your knowledge to customize the buying and selling processes to create your own personal selling system. This step is important in becoming a successful sales professional because it focuses your attention on the

buyer's particular situation and enables you to ask the right questions, offer the right solution, and manage the complexity of the buyer–seller relationship.

Section 3: How to Become a Trusted Advisor

- **Step 7: Accelerate Revenue.** Becoming a trusted advisor involves a team all rowing in the same direction. Without organizational support, your own company can become the biggest barrier in your selling success. This chapter discusses the many roles involved in a sales professional's job, as well as how to effectively manage expectations both internally with your manager and externally with your clients.
- **Step 8: Communicate Effectively.** Salespeople spend most of their time communicating, and often the content of their communication is highly repetitive. This repetition can lead to communicating without really thinking about the quality of the communication. Understanding all facets of communication can propel average salespeople to the top of the sales rankings—and this chapter focuses on the key concepts and tips to help get you there, including minimizing noise, polishing your questioning techniques, and mastering verbal and nonverbal communication skills.
- **Step 9: Manage Your Sales Organization.** Sales professionals have accountability and responsibility for driving revenue and must excel at the many roles they play within the buyer–seller relationship. In this step, sales professionals need to maximize their time investment, effectively run productive meetings, and skillfully maneuver within the sales culture of their organizations.
- **Step 10: Develop World-Class Sales Competency.** The most successful sales professionals are passionate about lifelong learning and never rest on their laurels or skills—instead, they continually focus on improving themselves and developing knowledge and skills. This chapter defines sales competencies and discusses strategies for closing sales and protecting your accounts.

Review these 10 steps as often as needed to help you transition from salesperson to sales professional and attain trusted advisor status with your clients.

Additional Value: Sales Gurus and Worksheets

Interwoven throughout the book you'll see quotes from real-world "gurus" who offer their sage advice and best tips. These sales professionals serve as guides on your journey throughout the process.

Worksheets at the end of each step will help you apply the key concepts discussed, such as defining what success means to you, revisiting your beliefs about the sales profession, identifying the actions you should take when applying the Continuous Sales Improvement Cycle, and more.

SECTION ONE

OVERVIEW

How to Be Effective

To get off to a quick start you must have focus and take action quickly. Your ability to accomplish the right tasks at the right time will allow you to make an impact quickly. And your ability to know where you are and (more important) know what you need to accomplish next are keys to becoming a world-class sales professional. This requires you to master the art of sales effectiveness.

Sales effectiveness is defined as something that is adequate to accomplish a purpose or something that produces the intended or expected result. Simply put, sales effectiveness is about accomplishing set goals. It is gained by knowing *what you need to do.* This level of understanding comes from

- Step 1: Embrace a Sales Mindset
- Step 2: Know Your Job and Your Role
- Step 3: Develop Winning Habits

A Sales Professional is an effective and efficient trusted advisor.

STEP ONE

Embrace a Sales Mindset

OVERVIEW

- Know and embrace your responsibility
- Constantly take inventory
- Understand your personal selling style
- Produce the right results
- Understand the continuous improvement cycle

I am very interested in helping you become a better sales professional quickly. I don't want you to become a sales professional 20 years from now—I want you to become a sales professional as soon as you're ready. Many sales managers I talk to realize that there is a difference between a salesperson and a sales professional. Sales *people* attempt to study sales closing techniques and sale steps, but sales *professionals* don't stop there. They continue to study the science of selling. How do you know when you are a sales professional? Your customers tell you and they treat you like one!

Selling is not simply about encouraging someone to buy a product or service; it is also about listening, analyzing, problem solving, and persuasion. Selling is about valuable conversations and relevant communications designed to help you move the sales process forward by becoming a trusted advisor.

Did you know that the word *sell* is derived from the Icelandic word *selja* and the Anglo Saxon word *syllan*—both of these mean "to serve" or "to give"? Sales professionals often recommend solutions

STEP 1

that will ultimately help organizations and individuals become more successful and achieve their goals. Therefore, as a sales professional, you must realize that you have a large amount of responsibility and accountability for your actions.

A sales professional is an effective and efficient trusted advisor.

Professional actions and outputs help you focus on one aspect of becoming a world-class sales professional—sales effectiveness.

Simply put, sales effectiveness is about accomplishing set goals. Sales effectiveness is gained by knowing *what you need to do.* This level of understanding comes from:

- embracing a sales mindset
- knowing your job
- developing winning habits.

Know Your Responsibility

No matter how you look at it, you have a huge responsibility to live up to. Your success is ultimately your company's success. And as you embrace that responsibility, you'll have more support and more power internally (with your organization) and externally (with your customers). As your level of responsibility and involvement in your company increases, you will have greater opportunities to co-create more complex solutions with more and more customers. This means you will develop a substantial amount of experience and expertise, which are needed to drive *even more* revenue. In other words, you must keep increasing your performance, you must continue to build your client base, and you must continuously improve over the long term. I have

POINTER

Diagnosing the customer's needs before launching into a soliloquy about yourself or your firm's scope is crucial to properly positioning your product or service. Approaching the sales process with this mindset will arm you with a patience and curiosity that will separate you from the competition.
– Brian Dunn, Director of Business Development, OPTIMBUY Consulting

met salespeople who think they "know everything"—but they stop being effective, their customers' knowledge becomes greater than their own knowledge, and they usually find themselves unhappy with their occupation. Don't let that happen to you!

As a sales professional, you could be responsible for the development and implementation of selling strategies for specific brands or you could support a number of key strategic accounts in a focused manner. Typically new sales professionals, depending on experience, start with accounts that are "less complex." With this type of customer, your organization is saying, "If we lose one of these accounts because the salesperson screws up, it is OK." Initial assignments typically include the implementation of selling strategies that allow you to build competency. Over time, you will gain more exposure and responsibility with larger customers and you will participate in strategy development as well as strategy implementation—besides just tactical selling. You just have to pay your dues first.

Embrace Your Accountability

With increased responsibility comes accountability. You must first build a bridge of accountability by being trustworthy and possessing professional expertise and poise. In other words, the best way to be accountable is to increase your knowledge and skill. Accountable salespeople are characterized by trustworthiness, integrity, and competency. Competency is built through accountability for your actions, accountability with your customers, and accountability with your own company.

> **POINTER**
> Always ask first before you tell. After all, people buy for their reasons, not yours.
> *– Jake Atwood, President, Ovation Sales Group*

Responsibility and accountability lead to effectiveness. And your effectiveness is judged based upon your behavior and your overall impact on the success of your organization. Goal setting, performance management, attention to detail, and team-building skills provide the foundation of effectiveness, while taking initiative, inspiring, setting an example, delegating, coaching, creating, learning, coordinating, and acting strategically are demonstrable aspects of effectiveness.

Constantly Take Inventory

To become a top sales performer, you must start by knowing yourself. This helps you to "serve" or "give" your talents to clients in return for a transaction. No matter how long you've been in the profession, it is important to periodically assess the type of salesperson you currently are and who you want to become. Even if you don't have it all figured out, it's important to keep looking at yourself in the mirror.

In professional selling, there are many indicators of how good you are. Most of those indicators have to do with numbers. This is because the amount of revenue you bring to a company can be easily quantified. However, to be a successful seller, you should strive to emulate or improve your actions, as well as maximize your own strengths and minimize any weaknesses.

To do this means that you need to objectively determine:

- What results am I currently achieving?
- What results are desired of me?
- How large is the gap between my current performance and my expected performance?
- What is the impact of that gap on me, on my employer, and on others?

If there is a gap in performance, then the goal is to clearly understand why the gap exists. Perhaps you don't have the right information, support, or time/ability to perform all of the work that needs to be done. At times, the "rewards" in place do not provide the proper incentives. These are all examples of "external factors" that cause the performance gap—all of which are outside of your control (and are usually the purview of the management team).

How do you close the controllable gap in performance? You focus on honing your competence—your knowledge, skills, and abilities in becoming a trusted advisor.

POINTER

Your customer's customer is your customer too. Help them increase their sales and they will increase yours.
– Antoine Loup, International Sales and Information Systems, Insulating Coatings Corporation

Think about a time when you bought something very valuable. What was the role of the salesperson in that buying experience? Was he or she a salesperson or a sales professional in your opinion? If you have had the opportunity to meet great sales professionals, what did you observe about them? What behaviors did they embody that you should strive for? In general, the behaviors of great sales professionals can serve as a guide for you and may include

- honesty
- ethical standards
- integrity
- ability to build trust
- credibility
- effective time management
- in-depth product knowledge
- competitor knowledge
- passion for lifelong learning.

For example, sales professionals who are honest and ethical can build trust with their customers quickly. But there is a balance. Because sales professionals are more honest and ethical in their approach, they may be perceived (by other salespeople) as not making sales happen as quickly as they should (which is probably a misperception of what is really true). Remember, not only do honesty and integrity build trust and net long-term customers, but they also go a long way in smoothing over issues or situations when hiccups occur. Clients who truly like their salespeople and view them as professional are often much more willing to work through issues rather than bail on the relationship at the first bump in the road.

Understand Your Personal Selling Style

When I talk with new salespeople, I often ask them about their selling style. Their answers usually involve their understanding of the product, technical aspects of their service, their awareness of the industry, or their overall understanding of the profession. While it's true that selling style is influenced by the knowledge you gain, it also involves your values, personality traits, and motivations. Understanding your personal style is important. But it's how you use your personal selling style that really matters.

For example, John is a salesperson who values money and the need for achievement. As a result, his style drives him to want to "make the sale" or win an award. In contrast, Sue's selling style is more introspective and analytical. As a result, her style may lead her to a different type of sale that is more complex and requires more buyer education. Think about the type of seller you are, and understand the best sales job for you. There are sales positions out there that will fit your specific style!

Know Your Sales Style

One key component of your sales style is your personality type. You can identify your personality type and traits through various types of tests, such as the Myers-Briggs Type Indicator, which can help you understand what makes you tick and may define the type of sales job that best suits your interests and innate competencies.

For example, if you

- require immediate satisfaction and gratification, then product-oriented selling may be right for you.
- are a "system thinker" and analytical, then complex solution selling across the entire organization may be right for you.
- like building relationships and relating to people, you might want to consider more of a "farmer" role within existing accounts as opposed to the "hunter" role that requires you to dig up new business.

What is it that great salespeople know and do that makes them successful? The key begins with what great salespeople know about themselves. To start, great salespeople understand that

- their inner thoughts affect their behavior—particularly when selling.
- they should behave in a professional manner even when under stress and in situations that might illicit unproductive behavior.
- their outward personalities impact their communications and selling approaches with their customers.
- how their customers perceive them—both positively and negatively—will impact their effectiveness.
- they may need to adjust their styles to sell more effectively to customers with similar or different styles.

Great sales professionals also maintain a positive mental attitude no matter what comes their way. They view client objections as an opportunity to continue discussions and further educate clients on why their products and services are the best solution to meet their business needs.

Regardless of what type of selling style you exhibit, a fundamental take away in developing your sales mindset involves selling *your own* way to maximize *your* strengths. For example, if you are analytical, then sell with a more analytical approach. You don't have to come outside of your comfort zone to be successful in the sales profession.

Produce the Right Results

No matter what selling style you have, you must "fit the mold" of a sales professional. While all sales professionals have accountability, responsibility, and a personal style, they also possess the ability to align their activity to get the job done. They never seem to forget that the definition of success is the ability to drive results.

Now this may seem obvious, but results don't "just happen." If sales results were easy, then more people would be willing to become salespeople. Experienced sales professionals produce results

STEP 1

> **POINTER**
>
> Consistency, consistency, consistency. The cornerstone to any successful sales career is to apply what you've learned and be consistent about it. Visit your clients or prospects regularly. Follow up regularly and respond with a sense of urgency always.
> *– Michael J. Telesky, Senior Sales Executive, United Healthcare Specialty Benefits*

and outputs that are different from an entry-level salesperson for several reasons. Understanding that you need to produce results and outputs will help you become a more trusted advisor with your colleagues and customers. For example, experienced sales professionals are able to adapt better, think on their feet quicker, and be creative because they realize their actions lead to results. The more focused and appropriate the action, the better the result. Further, experienced sales professionals understand that there is an intermediate dynamic *between* their actions and results: that is, outputs. Outputs, whether tangible or intangible, are what successful salespeople produce or provide to colleagues, customers, and clients.

Figure 1.1 shows how actions relate to personal outputs and sales results.

What actions, outputs, and results distinguish great sales professionals?

Actions (observable behaviors):

- follow a written sales plan
- take responsibility for their own actions
- define and follow a personalized sales process that means something to them

FIGURE 1.1

How Results Are Achieved

- consistently and effectively prospect in the most appropriate manner
- reach the appropriate decision maker
- listen effectively
- use questions effectively
- bond and build rapport with others
- uncover hidden or latent needs and budgets
- display a strong desire for success
- display unwavering commitment to do what it takes
- are positive in relationships with others
- cultivate a positive and optimistic outlook
- possess a strong sense of self-confidence
- understand personal beliefs and values
- control emotions
- do not need approval from others
- handle rejection from others
- are able to talk about business and the financial arrangements of a deal

Outputs (something tangible or intangible that is produced or provided to others):

- produce sales results
- produce proposals or quotes that are well thought out
- provide accurate forecasts of deals pending
- produce written goals

Results (measurable or quantifiable outcomes):

- achieve quotas
- get commitments and decisions
- develop strong relationships with clients and customers
- garner respect of colleagues and peers

Continuously Improve

One of the traits of successful sales professionals is a passion for continuous improvement and learning. The *Continuous Sales Improvement Cycle* (CSIC) is a methodology I have used for 15 years. This approach helped me understand my role in relation to the buyer and become a more competent salesperson by understanding my strengths and weaknesses. I used the CSIC for everything from diagnosing weaknesses in my approach to crafting and co-creating customer solutions. I even used it to help my customers overcome their unique challenges.

To improve constantly, you need a way to repeatedly examine strengths and weaknesses, enable a change in your performance gap, and take the appropriate action to help close the gap. The CSIC is an effective tool to do just that. As shown in Figure 1.2, the CSIC has five phases and can be remembered as the "5Es":

Phase 1: Explore—In this phase, the goal is to explore a situation from every possible angle. It is important that you separate yourself and think strategically and tactically about the problem, challenge, solution, process, or project. No matter what you are exploring, you will need to clearly assess your strengths, weaknesses, and opportunities.

Phase 2: Examine—In this phase, the goal is to examine the specific need you're trying meet. You must work hard to clearly and specifically identify what strategic or tactical problem needs to be solved and align your work and results to fill clearly identified gaps. It is helpful to have a written plan that documents your intended course of action. Remember to focus on what outputs or results you need to achieve and document the tools, resources, strategies, and actions you will use.

Phase 3: Enable—In this phase, the goal is to enable your plan from the previous step and think about what it will take to put it into action. While the plan may look flawless on paper, rarely does it ever roll out in the manner that was intended (think of a standard sales process!). Brainstorm as many different scenarios as possible.

Phase 4: Engage—In this phase, the goal is to actively pursue your course of action. Here you complete tasks, finish processes, and meet your objectives. If things go awry, go back to the earlier phases and reengage the model (that's why it is cyclical).

FIGURE 1.2

The Continuous Sales Improvement Cycle (CSIC)

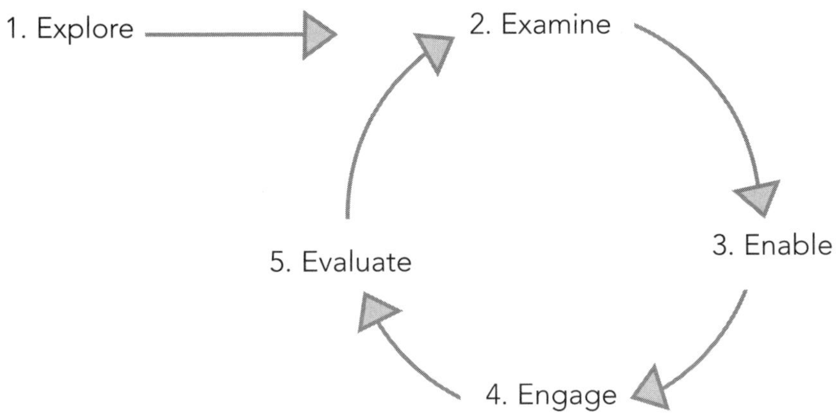

Phase 5: Evaluate—In this phase, the goal is to actively measure your progress and gather the feedback you need.

Note: This cycle is never over. It is meant to help you increase your agility in meeting organizational and market demands. As a result, you may need to reexamine, reenable, reengage, and reevaluate many times until you feel you have attained your objective.

The CSIC in Action: How Buyers Buy and Sellers Sell

The CSIC can help define the stages that both buyers and sellers progress through during the selling and buying processes.

Let's first consider the view through the "lens" of a buyer. The buying organization will

1. *explore* their personal and organizational needs
2. *examine* the options

3. *enable* their plan (research, examine options, etc.)
4. *engage* in a decision with one (or several) selling organizations
5. *evaluate* their success with the purchase.

Now let's examine the sales perspective. All sales professionals (and their selling organizations) progress through the same elements when selling products or services. The selling organization will

1. *explore* the needs of potential buyers
2. *examine* the options of positioning against the need of the potential buyers
3. *enable* their plan (how they will sell, plans, and so on)
4. *engage* in a decision (engage in the marketplace)
5. *evaluate* their success with the sale.

Sales professionals using the CSIC model build a solid understanding of the profession because it offers a universally applicable approach to defining the buying and selling relationship. Obviously, though, this process does not end here. An all-encompassing view that drills down several levels deeper into the activities and framework of selling is found later in this book.

When starting any new job, it is important to understand exactly what is expected of you in order to meet or exceed the expectations. Oftentimes, these expectations are not explicit—meaning your goals may be loosely defined—and are nearly impossible to achieve since measures and benchmarks are vague or nonexistent. The next chapter focuses on the four key benefits of the sales profession, how organizations define sales strategies and market segmentation, and the seven functions of any sales job. After you clearly understand your organization and your boss' expectations of you, the next step in the process involves developing winning habits to help you progress from a salesperson to a sales professional and trusted advisor.

POINTER

Don't give up until the prospect tells you to remove his number from your lists. People are busy and even if they want your product or service, the timing may not be right. Don't give up.
– Steven Menconi, Regional Sales Director, A Choice Nanny

WORKSHEET 1.1

Planning for Selling Success Leveraging the CSIC

When starting a new job or when new products are added to your portfolio, you will have many items and services to learn about. The same is true if your company is rolling out a new product and you need to understand how to sell the solution. Use this worksheet to apply the CSIC model to any new or existing product that you need to learn more about.

Phase	Your Actions
Phase 1: Explore	What I need to do: ◆ List all the ways that this solution is designed to help fill specific needs. ◆ List the unique aspects of the industry(s) in which my solution can help. ◆ Brainstorm who can help me. Find out their job titles, what are their needs, etc. ◆ Think about what else is important for me to know. *Note: If you get stuck, ask your manager to help.*
Phase 2: Examine	What I need to do: ◆ Find out what competitors are attempting to fill the same need. ◆ Discover what additional information I need and where can I get it in regard to products that buyers may be considering. ◆ Determine who else internally can help. ◆ What else is important for me to know? *Note: If you get stuck, ask your manager to help.*
Phase 3: Enable	What I need to do: ◆ Create a unique selling proposition or "elevator pitch" about my solution. ◆ Create a sales presentation. ◆ Identify potential questions the buyer may have. ◆ Determine what else I need to do to prepare. *Note: If you get stuck, ask your manager to help.*
Phase 4: Engage	What I need to do: ◆ Make a sales call. ◆ Create a proposal. ◆ Follow the sales process. ◆ Answer customer inquiries. ◆ Brainstorm additional actions in this phase. *Note: If you get stuck, ask your manager to help.*

continued on next page

Worksheet 1.1, continued

Phase	Your Actions
Phase 5: Evaluate	What I need to do: • Discover what worked. • Find out what didn't work and why. • Determine what I should start doing differently. • Determine what I should stop doing. • Determine what additional strategies I can employ. *Note: If you get stuck, ask your manager to help.*

NOTES

Know Your Job and Your Role

OVERVIEW

- Know the goals expected of you and how you are paid
- Know how to do the "sales math"
- Know how sales strategies are created
- Know your portfolio and the types of sales positions
- Know the seven functions of any sales job

Think about an activity you enjoy. Why do you enjoy it? Is it because you are good at it, because it comes easy for you, or because it enables you to explore your creativity while providing satisfaction? Now think about the jobs you have had. Did you enjoy them as much as the activity? Did they come as easy or provide as much satisfaction?

The Satisfaction of Selling

Why do people pursue careers in the sales profession? A sales career can provide many rewards and benefits. It can be fast-paced, challenging, and enable you to have a great deal of responsibility and autonomy to meet quotas and generate revenue. For the most part, you are your own boss in determining how much effort you make and how you spend your time. In fact, many consider selling to be a great occupation with many perks—which is largely due to four key components:

- **Personal satisfaction**—most salespeople have a high level of satisfaction with their jobs. This comes from achieving goals, being autonomous, helping clients meet business needs or overcome challenges, making people happy, and receiving high pay.

- **Personal control**—most sales professionals have control over their own destiny when it comes to driving revenue for their organizations, influencing product features, and handling customer service concerns and fulfillment issues. They also have significant control over their own schedules and how much money they make.
- **Serving others**—if you think about it, selling is also a service profession. Sales professionals derive great satisfaction from helping clients and companies succeed. They also embrace challenges and complaints as opportunities to help.
- **High compensation**—sales professionals are some of the highest paid people in the world. This compensation is based on attaining a high level of performance. The sales profession is one of the few where the harder you work, the more money you can make. This "control your own destiny" approach appeals to those who have a desire to win and are motivated by high achievement.

STEP 2

Get Started: What You Need to Know

When transitioning from salesperson to sales professional, there are several key things you should know—which many professionals are unaware of until they have accumulated years of experience or when an unforeseen "gotcha" rears its ugly head. To avoid these situations, use the following list as a guide to get the answers you need early in your sales career.

Know the Goals Expected of You

One of the most important things you need to know is what the company and your boss expect from you. Granted, they want you to be successful and make money for the company and for yourself personally—but there are many other aspects of the job they don't tell you; for example, be professional, be on time, achieve specific goals in the territory, and so on.

One of your first missions in beginning any new sales position should be to uncover exactly what is expected of you from both the company and your boss' perspectives. In addition to understanding expectations, every successful sales professional has mastered the following basic laundry list of skills:

- company-specific information
- industry knowledge
- product knowledge
- selling skills (such as prospecting and negotiating).

Know How You Are Paid

This may seem basic, but many times salespeople sign on for a job and the exact structure of the compensation plan from which they will be paid is a bit murky. Caution! You really need to know and understand how you are paid.

Compensation plans should be designed to specifically reward results. In other words, they are usually crafted in a way that helps the organization achieve certain business objectives. If the organization is focused on entering a new territory, launching a new product, or retaining existing customers, the management team will usually draft a compensation plan designed to reward salespeople for helping the organization achieve these business objectives.

Compensation plans can be composed of a fixed component (such as a salary) or a variable component (commission or bonus). Between the fixed and variable components, the compensation plan could get tricky. For example, the variable portion could contain accelerated rates, extra bonuses, or payouts that need to be calculated. The key for you is to

> **POINTER**
> Passion is power. Belief in yourself and your product can open any door.
> – *Paul B. Novick, Sales Manager*

STEP 2

understand what the variable portion of your compensation plan rewards and align yourself accordingly. To help salespeople stay focused, the compensation plan is often broken down into more manageable chunks. These "quotas" or "goals" are handed to salespeople as a set of yearly, monthly, and (sometimes) weekly targets for revenue creation. It's important that you know and understand your quota and how it ties into your compensation plan. More important, it's crucial to do the math and figure out the level of activity and effort you need to attain your set quota.

Know How to Do the "Sales Math"

Part of understanding your compensation plan requires you to know your quota for the year. While knowing it is one thing, attaining it is another. To help you attain your quota, you should break it down into a very specific set of actions. Consider the following guidance:

- How many phone calls or contacts does it take to lead to a qualified prospect?
- How many qualified prospects does it take to lead to a proposal?
- How many proposals does it take to lead to a sale?
- How many sales does it take to attain your quota?

These actions are measurable and can provide you with a great gauge to help achieve your quota. Newer salespeople may find that they require more phone calls, more prospects, and more proposals than their experienced colleagues. Approach this process with the mindset that you will need to consistently improve over time.

Know How Sales Strategies Are Created

Many times, salespeople have a misperception of what the job will entail because they do not fully understand the sales strategy employed by their organization. Understanding how these strategies are created will help you determine where you fit within the sales organization and what to do to be successful.

While there are several types of sales positions, companies typically decide which positions they need by first understanding their sales strategy and how they want to be perceived in the market. To help you understand the decisions your organization made, consider the following:

- How much face-to-face time does my management team believe is necessary to gain and retain customers?
- What types of activities does my management team believe lead to increased buyer trust?
- What is the position of my company in relation to the competition in the marketplace?
- What specific sales actions does my management team believe will maximize the firm's growth plans?

POINTER

Three keys to successful selling:

Commitment—You must be committed to what you are doing. Customers can sense the degree of intensity and passion you project in your speech and body language. If you truly believe in what you are doing, customers will sense it and they will be more likely to give you their business.

Persistence—You must be persistent in your daily activities without being overbearing. Self-discipline is a key component of persistence. Do the things you need to do everyday to be successful.

Perseverance—You will get five times more "nos" than "yeses." Each "no" gets you closer to the next "yes."

– Jim Clark, President, Clark Consultants

As an example, based on analyses of these four questions, your management team decides to employ a sales strategy composed of essentially two components:

- **Sales territories** will be used to determine the scope of the salesperson's reach within the market.
- **Sales positions** will be used to help the organization achieve the sales results set.

To determine the size of the sales territory and types of sales positions needed, your management team must have a solid

STEP 2

understanding of the market. The market is defined as the entire universe of available prospects for your company's product or service. To understand the market, your management team may utilize focus groups, surveys, customer feedback, and so on. Based on this knowledge of the market, the *complexity* and *size of the sale* of the product or service will be determined.

- **Complexity** is defined by the number of decision makers needed to make a purchase, as well as the number of different functions (such as finance, IT, marketing, and training) that need to sign off on the purchase.
- The **size of the sale** is determined by the average investment (as determined by time and cost) needed by a customer.

Therefore, the types of positions needed in the sales organization are based on the buyer. A larger size deal (in the eyes of the buyer) will require more time for implementation and cost more than a smaller size deal.

For example, XYZ Company sells highly complex, multimillion-dollar enterprise resource planning (ERP) software. In this type of sale, many decision makers are involved from the buying organization and a sale entails many different departments to sign off on the purchase of the software.

How does the selling organization determine the number of salespeople to employ? In this situation, the selling organization would employ a direct sales strategy (as opposed to indirect sales) where they decide how to segment their sales efforts and the types of sales roles based on the complexity and size of the sale.

POINTER

If you find yourself saying, "That's not my job," (1) it probably is your job and (2) you're focusing on the wrong thing in the first place.
– Brian Lambert, Director, ASTD, Sales Training Drivers

STEP 2

Complexity of Selling Products, Services, and Add-Ons

Selling products is different from selling services—and selling many products bundled together is more complex than selling just one product. Obviously, selling an entire solution across many different departments is different than selling just one product. **Product sales** involve selling anything that can be considered a commodity. A commodity is a generic, largely unprocessed good that can be packaged and, many times, resold. Examples include off-the-shelf software, hardware, or network components; copy machines; or fax machines. Many commodities can be bundled together if needed by the customer.

Service sales involve selling consulting or training services to the customer. A service is anything involving the implementation, training, or servicing of a product. Service sales can also be "pure services," such as consulting or financial services (banking, investing, and so on) or professional services, such as medicine or law. Believe it or not, one of the biggest challenges facing law firms today is the ability to sell their professional services.

A **solution** is a combination of products and/or services that completely solves the needs of the customer. A solution can be defined as anything the selling organization has that can solve the problems of the buying organization. Therefore, the definition of a solution is driven by the customer, not the selling organization. For example, a salesperson who sells paper to a business may think he or she is selling a product, but this doesn't completely solve the customer's problem of creating an annual report to ship to 100,000 people. The more complete the solution, the more complex it becomes.

Many product companies also have services that can be added on to the sale. **Add-on sales** are anything that salespeople can up-sell to an original sale in order to provide a more complete solution. For example, if a salesperson sells antivirus software, an add-on could be firewall software to provide a more robust solution to securing data. If a salesperson sells antivirus and firewall software, an up-sell might be a server to contain all of the data—a different product line, but part of an overall solution.

STEP 2

Know Your Portfolio

Your territory is the geography area where you can find prospects and convert them to wildly happy, long-term clients. To sell a product or service, an organization has to decide on the segmentation strategy needed. Segmentation is defined as the slicing and dicing of a market to form territories. When the market is segmented, the organization will be able to determine the best strategy to cover the resulting territories, such as a mix of direct or indirect sales strategies. There are four ways to segment a market to define territories:

Geographic segmentation is straightforward and involves defining a territory based on

- country (such as the entire United States)
- region (such as the Northeast or Southwest)
- state (or mixture of states)
- city (or major metropolitan area).

Account segmentation is accomplished by assigning an account to a specific person or team. This can be done by using the size of the account (total revenue from the account) or by the first come, first served basis.

Vertical market segmentation is accomplished by grouping all accounts within one area of specialty by the types of customers, including:

- business-to-business (or B2B)—businesses that sell to other businesses
- business-to-consumer (B2C)—businesses that sell to consumers
- business-to-government (B2G)—businesses that sell to federal, state, or local governments
- business-to-association (B2A)—businesses that sell to non-profit and for-profit trade or charity associations.

Channel segmentation involves using a distribution channel (companies that resell a product) to reach customers. Channel marketing consists of developing go-to-market plans, educating channel marketers, and motivating the members of the marketing channel to promote products and services. An example of this would be a company that sells Hewlett-Packard software and hardware bundled within their solution.

Know the Types of Sales Positions

STEP 2

Professional selling occurs through several types of communication and interaction strategies. Each of these sales strategies has unique aspects that make it relevant for particular selling situations.

As depicted in Figure 2.1, there are two primary groupings of selling strategies—direct channels and indirect channels. A channel is how the company decides to go to market and sell its products or services. Every organization must make a choice on how to sell—

FIGURE 2.1

Direct and Indirect Selling Channels

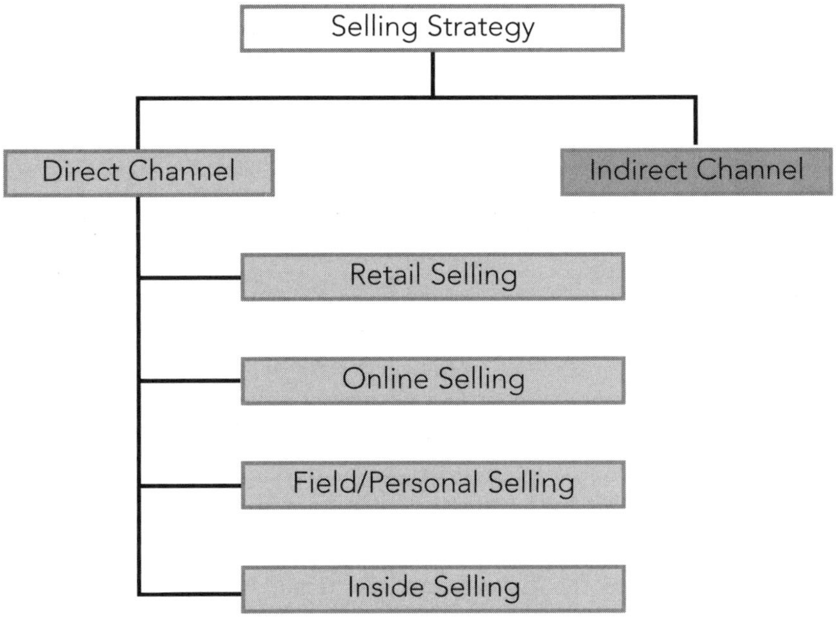

that is, either directly to the end user (usually with some sort of "point of sale" enabler, such as a salesperson) or indirectly through a reseller, partner, or alliance.

Indirect sales channels as part of professional selling are big business. Indirect sales organizations do not deliver a product or service to an actual end-user of that product. For example, Hewlett-Packard's primary business is selling computers and printers. To provide a complete solution to customers, they may provide consulting services via subcontractors—that is, an indirect sales channel.

The other channel in Figure 2.1 represents direct sales. In direct sales, there are four primary selling strategies that organizations may use to sell products or services directly to the end-user, including retail sales, online sales, using a field or personal selling, or inside sales strategies.

Know the Seven Functions of Any Sales Job

The selling environment is complex! Many different forces at work require a successful salesperson to skillfully juggle the demands of his or her own company with the requirements of the client. To do this, you must understand different sales functions, how they relate to various aspects of the sales process, and the traits required to successfully perform in each job.

There are seven primary functions of highly competent sales professionals as detailed in Table 2.1. These functions build on each other with two critical functions being the "Positioner" and the "Catalyst," illustrated in Figure 2.2. This is because the Positioner bridges the gap between marketing and selling, and the Catalyst bridges the gap between sales and service as well as maintaining focus on a unique transaction.

In analyzing these functions, it is helpful to identify the primary focus of each function and the general expectations for its role during the pre-sale and post-sale phases. If you are currently in sales or aspire to land your first job in the profession, how will

(*Text continues on page 30.*)

TABLE 2.1

Seven Functions of Sales Professionals

STEP 2

Function	Description
Strategic Planning	• Responsible for fact finding with key individuals inside the selling organization and lead the internal efforts to create an appealing message that a buyer will understand and appreciate. This role requires a solid understanding of corporate strategy and buyers to develop a comprehensive solution that fills their needs and meets their expectations in order to hand it off to the "Messaging" function. • **Required competencies for this function include:** strategic orientation, ability to see the big picture, and ability to tie long-term vision into short-term goals. Should be straightforward, highly intellectual, a problem solver, and a fact finder.
Client-Focused Messaging	• Focused on clearly identifying the key benefits a specific buyer will purchase, as well as bridge the "marketing and selling" gap. • Seeks to understand selling organization's position in a prospect's mind and stays focused on understanding the prospect or client. • **Required competencies for this function include:** emotional strength, customer focused, creative, market oriented, strategic, conscientious, and curious. Must also have the ability to improvise and take abstract ideas and make them concrete.
Communicating Persuasively	• Focused on presenting, questioning, and managing sales communications with a specific buyer. • Responsible for articulating the selling organization's recommendation, approach, response, plan, or strategy in clear terms. Needs to set appropriate expectations in an ethical way with the buyer so as to not overpromise the company's capability to deliver. • Defines and refines a buying need and opens dialogue with the buyer to validate that the selling organization can deliver what is being sold. • **Required competencies for this function include:** sociable, well versed in many different subjects, patient, tactful, adaptable, quick, articulate, poised, gracious, and humble when appropriate in this role.

continued on next page

Table 2.1, continued

Function	Description
Focused Seller	• Focused on driving a unique transaction as well as bridging the "sales to service" gap. • Responsible for being an agent of the selling organization and working in a consultative and participatory process to identify a client's or prospect's business issues and put a plan in place that solves those issues. • This is the only role that focuses solely on creating a unique transaction. Usually this role is coupled with one of the other roles. This salesperson is still a "catalyst," even if communicating, facilitating, positioning, or managing, because the role is still focused on creating transactions. • **Required competencies for this role include:** resilient, "does not take no" personally, above average ambition, willpower, and determination. Can easily approach strangers. High energy level, supreme self-confidence, hunger for achievement (of power, money, prestige, or service) and the ability to see obstacles as challenges. Should be alert, courageous, inquisitive, persuasive, and sociable. **Note!** Many people believe that sales professionals are either "hunters" or "farmers"; however, they should always be "sellers." Sales professionals will be required to make something happen no matter which function is dominant.
Concerted Facilitating	• Almost exclusively focused on post-sale activities, including arranging for the implementation, installation, delivery, or other support for the mutually agreed-upon solution (product or service). • Facilitates the transfer of information, specifications, data, requirements, and other information to facilitate the deliverables necessary. This role serves as a communication coordinator to ensure that everyone involved (1) knows what they are supposed to do, or (2) is notified as customary to your organization. • **Required competencies for this function include:** personable, sensitive, open, precise, logical, level-headed, accommodating, consistent, and great attention to detail.

Table 2.1, continued

Function	Description
Managing Effectively	• Focuses on the entire process and ensuring goals are achieved. The effective manager is also focused on driving continuous selling cycle improvement initiatives. Fulfills administrative activities as well as tactical execution of a sales strategy. • Expected to be a great learner and teacher throughout the entire selling cycle. Responsible for influencing others in a positive manner internally in the selling organization, while maintaining high standards of personal health, time management, and action through daily activities. Needs to achieve management team expectations and execute revenue generation results effectively. • Creates measurements of success and uses technology to create appropriate reports, manage a defined process, forecast future sales, or collaborate to ensure your plans are progressing according to expectations. • **Required competencies for this function include:** accountable for results, dependable, loyal, obedient, strategic, empowering, and a problem solver. Must be intensely goal-oriented and have a commitment to current role and employer. Will have to be authoritative and direct if needed.
Value-Driven Advising	• Responsible for expanding new opportunities with existing relationships and protecting any relationships that exist from the competition. The primary focus of this role is to build relationships internally and externally that require the ability to build customer trust. • Must clearly understand when ethical issues arise and counter them accordingly. • **Required competencies for this function include:** working diligently to earn trust, build credibility, meet performance expectations, display belief in the selling organization and products or services sold, a successful track record, and professionalism.

FIGURE 2.2

Continuum of Sales Functions

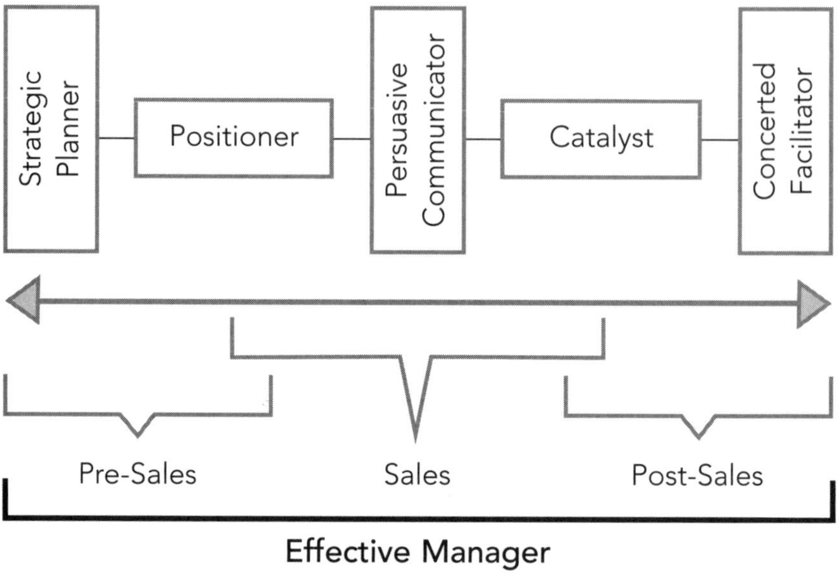

these roles "play out" as you perform your job? Do you see yourself spending more time in one function than another? What strengths and limitations do you currently have?

Once you have a better understanding of the types of functions you must execute in the sales profession, and how your job may change depending on whether you are more pre- or post-sale focused, you will need to learn what sales professionals do that make them successful.

The next step requires the ability develop winning habits—which in turn creates the foundation for becoming a highly competent sales professional! This aspect of selling and the habits required are discussed in Step 3.

WORKSHEET 2.1

Worksheet SMART Goal

Goal setting is more than simply scribbling down some ideas on a piece of paper. It involves complete focus on writing a statement that includes all of the elements of a "SMART" goal—that is:

S specific

M measureable

A achievable

R relevant

T time bound

In essence, your SMART goal should be a clear and specific statement of what you want. Use this worksheet to develop your goal statements to guide your path to selling success.

Instructions: List your top three SMART goals for the upcoming year.

Goal	Your SMART Goal Statement
Goal 1	
Goal 2	
Goal 3	

Instructions: Now that you've defined your three SMART goals, complete the worksheet below for each goal. A completed worksheet is provided for you as an example to help you get started.

Name: ______________________ Date: ______________

Goal	Your SMART Goal Statement
SMART Goal	To achieve $1.2 million in software sales by the end of 2010 by selling $300K of product X by April, $300K of services by June, and $300K of product Y by December.
BENEFITS of Achieving this Goal	I will enjoy increased pay through commissions and bonuses. I will build momentum for years of repeat business with these customers. I will feel a great sense of accomplishment in selling more product than in any other year. I will feel good about the job I am doing for my company—a place I like to work.

continued on next page

Worksheet 2.1, continued

STEP 2

Goal	Your SMART Goal Statement
STEPS of ACTION for Achieving this Goal	1. Update all my customers on our new product set by February 24. 2. Contact 100 new prospects by March 8. 3. Make appointments with all my existing customers to present recommendations by March 10. 4. Have first referral from a new customer by March 30. 5. Complete 25 web presentations by April 30.
Possible OBSTACLES	1. Letting a bottleneck develop by doing all my own implementation work. 2. Losing sales due to pricing concerns. 3. Losing sales due to installation issues.
Possible SOLUTIONS	1. Work closely with the marketing team to develop good marketing material. 2. Memorize pricing book BEFORE customers bring it up. 3. Solve problems with internal project management.

Name: ______________________________ Date: __________________

Goal 1	Your SMART Goal Statement
SMART Goal	
BENEFITS of Achieving this Goal	
STEPS of ACTION for Achieving this Goal	
Possible OBSTACLES	
Possible SOLUTIONS	

Worksheet 2.1, continued

Name: ____________________ Date: ____________

Goal 2	Your SMART Goal Statement
SMART Goal	
BENEFITS of Achieving this Goal	
STEPS of ACTION for Achieving this Goal	
Possible OBSTACLES	
Possible SOLUTIONS	

Name: ____________________ Date: ____________

Goal 3	Your SMART Goal Statement
SMART Goal	
BENEFITS of Achieving this Goal	
STEPS of ACTION for Achieving this Goal	
Possible OBSTACLES	
Possible SOLUTIONS	

STEP 2

NOTES

STEP THREE

Develop Winning Habits

OVERVIEW

- Create your action plan
- Know (and exceed) your quota
- Map your pipeline and close rate to your quota
- Determine your priorities
- Master other successful habits and strategies

A frequent rhetorical question in the sales team is, "Where did my time go?" Think about the activities that can gobble up the valuable time of a sales professional: meetings, paperwork, customer requests, sales calls, creating proposals, following up, putting out fires, building relationships, prospecting and filling your pipeline, creating reports, and so on. It's easy to get caught up in day-to-day work and forget to reflect on your actions. It is important to determine if you are spending your time wisely and identifying which activities are the most critical to achieving your goals.

For most salespeople, even a small and consistent change in activities can have a significant impact on productivity. For those new to sales or seasoned pros who have fallen out of their groove, this step focuses on examining the activities that add value and increase productivity so you can determine how to appropriately allocate your time.

POINTER

Always know more than your customer with respect to product knowledge. Building value in sales begins and ends with the product presentation, features, benefits, and customers' value of such.
– Dan Ziegler, Guru, Cavatori – The Truffle Hunters

STEP 3

As discussed briefly in Step 2, setting goals is extremely important to your success. Since properly set goals and objectives can be very powerful motivators, you need to know what is expected of you and the rewards you can expect to receive for achieving or exceeding the sales goals. You also need to know if there are any penalties for underachieving them! This section will help you create and verify the key components to make the right plan for your territory and personal success.

Before you start any journey, you need a map—in sales terms, you need a plan to hit your quota and drive revenue. Before beginning this journey, you first need to know where you are and then develop a plan for how to get to your destination. Begin by asking yourself some basic questions:

- Where are you compared to your goals right now?
- What are the organization's goals compared to yours?
- Are your goals aligned with those of the organization?

As soon as you have determined the answers to these three questions, you can begin mapping out your plan to grow revenue in your territory.

Create Your Sales Action Plan: A 7-Step Process

It's never too late to begin taking action—the key is to start! Use the following seven steps to determine the actions you need to take and how you're going to get to your goals. These steps may be tricky, so use Worksheet 3.1 on page 52 to guide you. If you get stuck, ask a manager or a trusted colleague for help.

Step 1: Know (and Exceed) Your Quota

The first tenet of being a sales professional is to exceed your quota. In other words, know your base quota, add 20 percent to it, and *believe* you can achieve it.

- **Key Point 1**—Being "at plan" (making quota) is your minimum accepted contribution to your company—aim higher.
- **Key Point 2**—Make sure your new quota is tied to your compensation plan. Find out how much money you will make when you hit your new quota, and make sure it aligns with your personal financial goals. If it doesn't, set your quota higher.

Step 2: Break It Down

Regardless if your quota is annual or quarterly, break it into monthly increments. For example, imagine your annual quota is $1.8M (including the 20 percent bump). Therefore, your quotas are:

- $450K quarterly—that is, $1.8M divided by 4
- $150K monthly—that is, $1.8M divided by 12.

Breaking a quota into increments enables you to more effectively plan your sales activity on a quarterly and monthly basis. Some industries break sales quotas into weekly increments as well.

Step 3: Map Your Pipeline and Close Rate to Your Quota

For this step, you need two pieces of data:

- your closing ratio rate (for example, 50 percent, 80 percent, etc.)—The closing ratio is calculated by taking the number of deals closed and dividing by the number of proposals sent.
- the estimated revenue for each deal in your pipeline—The pipeline typically begins when you identify a qualified prospect. Ask your manager what *qualified* means at your

company. Make sure you know when to put your deal into the pipeline.

For each deal, you will need to make an educated guess on the deal size. Obviously, the closer you are to the proposal stage, the easier it is to properly size up the deal (revenue).

Calculate your net pipeline by multiplying the value of each deal by the close rate. Take the value of the deals in the pipeline (by the expected close date) and subtract the estimated net pipeline revenue from your quota for the appropriate period. For example, a $22.5K net pipeline deal is estimated to close in March and your quota for March is $150K. Therefore, you will need an additional $127.5K in net pipeline revenue to meet the new quota you set.

This process provides a good estimate of the amount of new pipeline net revenue needed to meet quota for each week, month, quarter, and the year.

POINTER

As you progress through your first year in sales, it's important to build fundamental sales skills and knowledge that will give you a decent chance to succeed. If you want to attain breakthrough performance levels, keep your focus on building extraordinary relationships while helping your decision makers solve problems that your competition cannot!
– Joe Donna, President, Sales Oxygen

Step 4: Develop Your Sales Plan for the Year

With quota and net pipeline numbers in line, now begin the process of developing a sales plan. A sales plan details *what* you need to do to meet or exceed your quota for the year. In the next step, you will detail *how* you will achieve your sales plan. All you need to do is plug your quota, net pipeline, variance, and achieved numbers into a spreadsheet similar to the example shown in Table 3.1. Note: A blank worksheet is located on page 52.

Tip! Some salespeople prefer to include additional columns based on their compensation plans. Many organizations that sell

TABLE 3.1

Annual Sales Plan Example

Period	Quota	Net Pipeline	Variance	Achieved
Jan	150,000		150,000	
Feb	150,000		150,000	
Mar	150,000	22,500	127,500	
Q1 Totals	**450,000**	**22,500**	**427,500**	
Apr	150,000	85,000	65,000	
May	150,000		150,000	
Jun	150,000		150,000	
Q2 Totals	**450,000**	**85,000**	**365,000**	
Jul	150,000		150,000	
Aug	150,000	175,000	–25,000	
Sep	150,000	65,000	85,000	
Q3 Totals	**450,000**	**240,000**	**210,000**	
Oct	150,000	25,000	125,000	
Nov	150,000		150,000	
Dec	150,000	250,000	–100,000	
Q4 Totals	**450,000**	**275,000**	**175,000**	
Yearly Totals	1,800,000	622,500	1,177,500	

Annual sales plan definitions

- **Period**—the period of performance (week, month, quarter, year)
- **Quota**—the assigned quota, as described in previous steps
- **Net Pipeline**—the adjusted revenue total of deals in the pipeline with estimated close dates in the period listed
- **Variance**—the difference between quota and net pipeline; a negative number signifies that the net pipeline is more than the quota for the period detailed
- **Achieved**—the actual revenue booked (per your comp plan) during the period listed

STEP 3

several types of products or a blend of products and/or services have quota numbers depending on the product mix. In this situation, consider adding two or more columns for each header (for example, two quotas would require two quota columns, two net pipeline columns, and so on).

Step 5: Determine Your Priorities

Now that you know what you need to do, you have to find the fastest way to get there. One way to accomplish that goal is to identify the best way to allocate your time. When it comes to driving revenue, you can focus your time on nonrevenue-generating activities that fall outside of the sales process or on revenue-generating activities that can be directly tied to the sales process. It's important to note that some administrative tasks can be classified as nonrevenue generating; however, they are still important (such as filling out expense reports).

> **POINTER**
> If you want something different to happen, you have to be willing to do different things.
> *– Jonathan London, President, The Improved Performance Group*

In addition, you can focus your activities on the type of account relationship. Your organization might have different names for the various types of accounts, but I have found that using "A," "B," and "C" labels is universal. Even if your organization labels accounts differently, you can still analyze the priority of the relationship and focus your time more appropriately. Spend more time on "A" accounts and less time on "C" accounts. Ask your manager to help you identify the importance of the account relationships that you manage.

> One way to think about allocating time:
> The closer to the sale, the more important the activity!

Step 6: Execute Your Plan

Use your skills to identify prospects, qualify each relationship, and build customer trust—then close the sale!

Step 7: Master Other Successful Habits

Every successful sales professional has mastered successful habits—most of which weren't provided in a book, but learned through trial and error on the job. All managers expect their sales professionals to show up on time for meetings, be professional, think strategically, and execute tactically, as well as being creative but grounded.

What other successful habits propel sales professionals from average to top performer? This section provides tried and true strategies and habits that any sales professional can use to make very quick, results-oriented self-checks and keep focused on what is most important—driving revenue growth and spending less time doing it.

Following are the 14 habits and 15 strategies that helped me achieve success early in my career.

STEP 3

Sales Habit 1: Everything Matters

A key aspect of shifting from salesperson to sales professional involves your level of attention to details. While some salespeople may focus on "what really matters," sales professionals recognize their role in the growth engine of the organization, and also realize that their work today can come back to them (in a good or bad way) tomorrow. They view selling with a systems perspective and maintain their humility no matter how much money they make. Most important, sales professionals recognize that the small things matter, such as showing up on time, returning a phone call, reading the industry news, or even taking time out with the family. Small details—timing of a presentation, tone of voice, and even what you wear—can have a big impact.

POINTER

Clearly understand the word *but*. What a client says after this word is often what the salesperson needs to address clearly with his or her client. For example, "I like your product *but* it is too expensive for me." Break down the barriers to the "but" objection and you will have a better chance of getting the sale. Everyone uses the word *but* often in business and in everyday life. Understanding this word is a most powerful sales tool.
– *Robert Shay, Life Coach*

Sales Habit 2: Show Me the Value

To show the value of why clients should buy your products or services, you need to focus your energy on leveraging those things your company does extremely well—especially those products or services that add the most value to your customer. This is an area where you can increase revenue the most.

Differentiation is another key to showing value. What does your company do better than anyone else? What do you do better than anyone else? What can you and your company do together to add value for your customers and prospects?

STEP 3

Sales Habit 3: Develop Your Talking Points

After developing a solid value proposition, the next step involves developing talking points. Talking points aren't scripts, per se; however, they detail the key points of your value proposition for the position you are selling to—that is, your "target." For example, you will need to develop specific talking points to effectively target the CEO, COO, CSO, VP of Technology, VP of HR, and so on.

Since different roles within an organization have different perspectives, priorities, challenges, and "hot button issues," successful sales professionals customize the value proposition and have different slants on their talking points depending on the buyer.

POINTER

If I'm stressed out about needing to close THIS deal, it means that I don't have enough deals in the pipeline. In these cases, I always go back and start working on lead generation.
– John Caddell, Principal, Cadell Insight Group

For example, a CEO is usually focused on increasing the value of the company (shareholder value, if public; partner equity, if private). There are two ways the value of the company is increased: driving revenue up and/or driving costs down. Most CEOs are not necessarily concerned about the more detailed aspects of a product or service you are offering. However, the CIO might need to know more detail on the technical aspects of your solution. In essence, the conversation with the CIO might be very different than the conversation with the CEO, even though you might be discussing the same value proposition for the same solution.

> POINTER
> Choose your destiny before it chooses you.
> – *Nick Reddin, Business Development Manager, Manpower*

If you don't want to go head to head with your competition, find a unique market niche that your competition doesn't serve—and take advantage of being first to market for it. Focus on what you, your company, and your product or service does to add value to your customers and prospects.

Sales Habit 4: Get the Activity Going

"Activity begets results" is a key phrase that sales managers often quote for their teams. It's true as long as the activity is the *right* activity. How do you focus on the right activity to meet or exceed your personal goals or company quota?

Start with your top 10 former customers. Call them to see how they are doing. Ask them why they have not done business with you recently (this is a very valuable method to understand the customer's perception of your company). If there are any issues, work through them. If not, engage the customer. Get back in there. Work a deal. Get the relationship back on track.

You've probably heard that it is more expensive to get new customers than to keep the ones you have or have had recently. Focus on existing relationships—even if they need some mending.

Increase your number of cold calls! Cold calling is just a form of networking and is as simple as calling someone you know and

POINTER

Always be alert and ready for the right occasion, dress right, talk right, and sell the right product to the right need.
– Taleb M. Hammad, Dr. Mortar and Pestle Pharmaceutical Marketing Company

STEP 3

having a conversation about their business. Everyone loves to talk about themselves! You do not need to close the sale; you just need to initiate the contact.

Look at any report that measures the correlation of sales success with the number of cold calls. The numbers don't lie. There is an absolute, direct connection between the number of cold calls and the success of a salesperson or sales team. The biggest barriers for most sales professionals in terms of cold calling are lack of skill, lack of preparation, and procrastination. Drive yourself to cold call. This is one habit that will *guarantee* your revenue growth.

Turn your cold calls into warm calls by understanding the target market and target customer (prospect). Before calling the boss to ask him or her about the company, find out for yourself. Research the target by getting an annual report, reading the company's website, and reviewing trade publications for the target's industry. After you've done your research, develop your value proposition and talking points specific to the target.

Following are additional ideas to get your creative juices flowing, but the key point is to get your name and your company in the market!

- Write newsletters, white papers, or position papers for existing and potential customers. Provide valuable information, free or low initial buy-in offers, or other perks to drive paid product or service business.
- Write for market-specific trade publications.
- Conduct short, value-focused seminars on increasing revenue or decreasing costs.
- Require your marketing department to get you qualified leads.
- Use your personal and professional networks.

Four Activity Keys to Grow Successful Sales

- **Be specific**—focus on how you can either reduce cost or increase revenue for your customer.
- **Think differently**—be unique and target the market differently than your competition.
- **Get noticed in your target market**—make some noise and show your value.
- **Ask**
  - for the opportunity to discuss (your value proposition)
  - for the opportunity to propose (your value proposition)
  - for the order
  - for the relationship to grow.

Sales Habit 5: Get Help Where Needed

The death knell to productivity for any sales professional is administrative duties. By leveraging technology wisely, salespeople get more time to sell and convert leads. Many basic types of sales automation tools have analytics capabilities that help track sales through a pipeline and enable you to define and establish sales reports and follow your progress toward achieving your quota. You don't necessarily need a high-end CRM (customer relationship management) system, just a way to record contacts, track progress, and report it in the most effective and efficient way, if your company has a CRM tool, use it. Leverage information technology or just have a process flow for hard copy reports.

The key is to define reporting parameters beforehand and make sure that you report in regularly. If your management does not require reporting, report anyway. The process of preparing reports requires that you fully qualify each opportunity and the probability of closure. Reporting also assists in setting priorities, which in turn saves valuable time for focusing on those opportunities that have the highest probability of closing.

If relevant, show management that having a sales administrator can help you increase revenue by X. Or reduce cost of sales by Y.

Use a metric that will show increased efficiency and value to the company that you couldn't provide on your own. A sales administrator could support more than one salesperson. Show value in real terms and you might get a favorable response.

Sales Habit 6: Leverage Your Strengths

There are two types of sales styles with regard to revenue growth—hunters and farmers—and these two styles exist in both inside and outside sales jobs.

Hunters are those salespeople who love the thrill of the new sale. As soon as they close the deal, they are on to the next—and they are very good at it. The main weakness of the hunter is that they typically do not nurture accounts; they lose interest in the account as soon as the deal is closed.

Farmers nurture accounts, but they typically don't penetrate new accounts. They take those accounts first closed by the hunters and expand them. Farmers close opportunity by opportunity, until they have sold all they can sell into that account. The weakness of the farmer is that the company they work for must continue to evolve and add new products and services, or the value of the farmer drops quickly.

The key is to understand the two sales styles and determine which role you do best. Exploit your strengths and find a partner who has complementary strengths so you can leverage each other. If you can do both hunting and farming, that's great! Find a sales job that fits your strengths.

Sales Habit 7: Commit to Be the Best

Win–loss reviews are one of the most valuable sales tools you can use. A win–loss review is an in-depth analysis of all aspects of the sales process for a particular deal. You need to look at each win and loss, and ask the sometimes-tough questions—the five Ws and and H (Who, What, When, Where, Why, and How). Basically, you need to review and understand what went right and what went wrong. Why did you win the deal (Win Review) or why did you lose the deal (Loss Review)?

As you review wins and losses, be sure to continuously scrutinize your pricing policy. If you are losing based on price, make sure you understand your sales process. If you sell based on value (realized value to the customer, not what you perceive your value to be), then you don't need to reduce the price. You might just need to work on your approach to communicating value to the customer.

Commit to be the best for your customers. This simple commitment to your key customers can provide huge returns. As you make this commitment to yourself, your boss, and your customer, impress upon everyone that you will do this by adding value to everything you do.

Making this commitment forces you to view all aspects of your customer's business and understand where you can help increase revenue and/or decrease cost. Focusing on your customer's business will not only help you grow revenue, but also increase your gross margin on every deal. If you stay committed and honest, this process will be the springboard for a long and profitable relationship between you and your customer.

Sales Habit 8: Determine What Your Customers Want and Need

Don't just look at what your customers want right now—determine what their needs will be in the future. Your customers may not know what their needs will be. Making it your mission to know the future needs of your customers will help you stay ahead of your competition.

Sales Habit 9: Take Your Executive Team on Sales Calls

The CEO of any company is usually the best salesperson. If you think your CEO is not a salesperson, you are wrong. How did the CEO get funding, hire the company's first staff member, or get the management team to accomplish business goals and objectives? Your CEO sold them all. Since the CEO owns the vision, who else can best sell their own vision?

Look at your sales pipeline and select the opportunity that is the largest in revenue, or the most profitable, or where you know the most about the customer/buyer. Set up a face-to-face meeting with a member of your customer's senior executive team, preferably the CEO.

Get the sale. This process affords you the opportunity to (1) get to know your executive team, (2) get to know the customer in a new light, (3) understand the issues in closing business today, and (4) gain confidence in what you and your company are doing, or need to do. You could be educating the executive on the sales team and sales process.

Sales Habit 10: Reduce Time Spent on Noncustomer Meetings

Unless internal meetings are absolutely necessary, immediately reduce the time spent on them. If the meetings must happen, then make them outside customer business hours. Every minute you are in an internal meeting, you are not in front of, on the phone with, or supporting the needs of a customer or prospect—meaning you are not adding value to the customer and you are diminishing your chances to generate revenue.

Sales Habit 11: Training Is Important, Even if You Have to Pay

Many sales professionals receive their training on the job via "trial by fire" or perhaps by being paired with a mentor. For many new professionals, this process often takes time to translate into correctly structuring smart deals and closing sales.

Most arguments against providing training for sales professionals revolve around the idea that training takes the salesperson out of the field. Salespeople themselves even reject having to go to sales training. Telling a salesperson they must attend training is perceived to be insulting—they think it means that they can't sell.

Leverage your sales skills to help strengthen the relationship between you and the rest of the company. For example, hold a series of "lunch and learn" sessions. Require attendance for at least one person from each department, if possible. The point is to give everyone the opportunity to participate. The focus of the training should be to educate the company on your sales process and get feedback from all employees on new ideas or approaches.

You may be surprised to discover where the best ideas come from. Remember to include all employees in the training sessions. The rewards will appear as revenue growth very quickly.

Sales Habit 12: Energize Alternate Channels

Sure you have partners. In today's networked world, everyone partners. Unlike others, though, make partnerships work for you. While you might not have the authority to execute contractual relationships, you can make personal commitments and team with many partners to drive your revenue growth.

If you have partners who aren't performing, reduce the amount of time you spend with them. Don't cut them off—you may need them at some point. However, the fact is, to get started in sales, you need revenue now. Focus on your customers and revenue-producing partners only.

Some examples of partnerships to consider include

- Resellers
- Agents
- Vendors
- Office suppliers
- Accountants
- Lawyers
- Event consultants

Sales Habit 13: Leverage Expert Resources

As a product- or service-based company, you should value your expert resources and place them at the top of your list of assets. Are you leveraging them to increase your revenue growth to the degree you should?

Have them

- prepare white papers
- give presentations at seminars or conventions
- attend pre- and post-sales calls
- run cross-project meetings
- build relationships with your customers and prospects.

Sales Habit 14: Leverage Your Back Office

Get everyone in the company involved in customer-related activities, including the back office. Many companies follow the "everyone sells" approach.

For example, have accounts receivable (A/R) meet with customers to

- pull in credit terms
- collect on slow players
- resolve invoicing issues
- understand the customer's best practices, processes, and procedures
- build relationships with your customers.

15 Strategies to Live By

1. Regulate your thoughts, wipe out worry, and rid yourself of resentment.
2. Nourish your mind with positive and uplifting thoughts.
3. Act the way you want to feel.
4. Remember—trouble finds everyone; keep perspective and focus on your response.
5. Take time to reflect before reacting to restore your sense of perspective.

6. Laugh a lot.
7. Learn from difficulty and seek opportunity in the difficulty.
8. Recharge relationships and seek solace from family and friends.
9. Lend a helping hand—helping others has been found to be the best medicine.
10. Keep going and don't get stuck in the difficulty; identify it and move on.
11. Waste less time.
12. Exercise regularly.
13. Contribute to your community.
14. Do not neglect your family or significant other in pursuit of the almighty dollar.
15. Focus on quality at every interaction.

Small and consistent changes in your activities can have a significant impact on productivity. Step 3 focused on examining the activities that add value and increase productivity so you can determine how to appropriately allocate your time. With the last step in the effectiveness section completed, Step 4 begins a new section on exploring sales efficiency and focuses on understanding the buying process, including how clients define value and make buying decisions.

WORKSHEET 3.1

Annual Sales Planning

Instructions: Use this worksheet to determine where you are with prospects and business in your pipeline and what you need to do to exceed your quota.

STEP 3

Calculate Your Monthly Quota

Multiply your annual quota by 1.20 (the .20 represents a 20% stretch goal).

Tip! Make sure that your new quota is tied to your compensation plan. Find out how much money you will make when you hit your new quota and make sure it aligns with your personal financial goals. If it doesn't, set your quota higher.

Divide that value by 12.

Enter the monthly value in the quota column for January–December cells.

Map Your Pipeline and Close Rate to Your Quota

Now, calculate your net pipeline by multiplying the value of each deal by the close rate (projected deal revenue × the close rate).

Calculate the Amount of New Pipeline Net Revenue Needed

Take the value of the deals in the pipeline (by the expected close date) and subtract the estimated net pipeline revenue from your quota for the appropriate period. Enter this value for the appropriate months in the net pipeline column.

Calculate Variance

Subtract the net pipeline value from the monthly quota numbers to determine the variance and how much business you need to win each month to meet or exceed your quota.

Period	Quota	Net Pipeline	Variance	Achieved
Jan				
Feb				
Mar				
Q1 Totals				
Apr				
May				
Jun				
Q2 Totals				

Worksheet 3.1, continued

Period	Quota	Net Pipeline	Variance	Achieved
Jul				
Aug				
Sep				
Q3 Totals				
Oct				
Nov				
Dec				
Q4 Totals				
Yearly Totals				

Annual sales plan definitions

- **Period**—the period of performance (week, month, quarter, year)
- **Quota**—the assigned quota, as described in previous steps
- **Net Pipeline**—the adjusted revenue total of deals in the pipeline with estimated close dates in the period listed
- **Variance**—the difference between quota and net pipeline; a negative number signifies that the net pipeline is more than the quota for the period detailed
- **Achieved**—the actual revenue booked (per your comp plan) during the period listed

STEP 3

NOTES

SECTION TWO

OVERVIEW

How to Be Efficient

Professionally approaching the buying and selling process helps you focus on a key aspect of your day: sales efficiency. Sales efficiency is defined as competency in performance. Simply put, it is about getting things done and can be improved by meeting the buyer right where they are at, following a standard sales process, and creating your own personal sales system.

Sales efficiency is gained by understanding how to approach the sales profession. It's not about what you know and it's not just how you go about it—it's about finding success within the sales process. This comes from

- Step 4: Understand the Buying Process
- Step 5: Leverage the Sales Process
- Step 6: Create Your Personal Sales System

A sales professional is an effective and efficient trusted advisor.

STEP FOUR

Understand the Buying Process

OVERVIEW

- Why do buyers buy?
- Understanding buyer expectations
- Defining value
- Getting to know the buyer
- Understanding negotiation strategies

Now that you have a better idea about what professional selling entails, this step focuses on what you need to do to be as efficient as possible. An efficient sales professional has the ability to join any sales organization, learn new product knowledge, and gain the trust of decision makers who manage the buying of products and services. They can also speak knowledgeably to various audiences—the CEO, front-line manager, or a new employee—about issues and challenges faced regardless of the vertical market. Obviously, product knowledge is absolutely crucial for selling success, but it is only one component necessary to customize a salesperson's approach with unique individual buyers. Specialization or "vertical focus" of skill is appropriate if you want to build expertise in a specific area; for example, IT application development sales.

Why Do Buyers Buy?

A question all salespeople ask at some point early in their career is, "Why do people want to buy from me?" There are two powerful reasons people want to buy: to move away from something (such as something that is costing the buyer a lot of money) or to move toward something (such as a future state that the buyer sees as a better option than the current situation).

Salespeople face continual challenges to satisfy more and more demanding buyers who have higher expectations. This dynamic creates a need for salespeople to approach the buyer–seller relationship not only from an employer's point of view, but also from the customer's. What exactly do buyers want from their sales professionals today? The answer to that question boils down to five key buyer expectations.

Buyer Expectation 1: Take More Responsibility

Buyers who are expected to make the right purchasing decisions want salespeople who work as partners to help them achieve business results. Howard Stevens, CEO of HR Chally, a sales consulting firm, says that buyers are "now demanding [that salespeople have] an understanding of their business, objective interpretation of their needs, and a more clear translation into implementation actions." Due to the evolution of buyer expectations, the knowledge, skills, and attitudes required by successful sales professionals are changing. Whereas in earlier times, salespeople were valued primarily for their persuasiveness and persistence, their abilities now must include strategic thinking, problem solving, active listening, and so forth.

Salespeople are under increased pressure to attain not only the goals of the selling organization, but the goals of the buying organization as well. This means that sales professionals must accept responsibility for ensuring success on both the buyer side and seller side of the relationship. Research conducted at the College of New Jersey explored the gaps in sales training content and delivery, and demonstrated that salespeople are *expected to ensure* reduced buyer logistics costs, higher standards of quality control, and greater mass-customization potential, and to act as problem solvers rather than pushers of standard solutions.

Buyer Expectation 2: Understand and Relate to the Business

Salespeople must continue to transition from transactional selling to relationship selling by adopting a true partnership mentality. Sales professionals need to strive more to become trusted advisors to their customers. They must develop deeper relationships and a personal network within customers' companies, while also developing networks and expertise within their specific industry. Tom Snyder, former president of Huthwaite, a salesforce improvement firm, suggests "salespeople need to probe for problems, needs, and opportunities that are top-of-mind for the buyer." As a result, salespeople should recognize that their products, typically seen as an area of differentiation, may be viewed as commodities by buyers. True differentiation involves demonstrating how the product will solve the buyer's business problems.

STEP 4

POINTER

Regardless of the industry or product you are selling, the thing a prospect has to buy first is you! Building personal rapport starts the moment prospects answer the phone or invite you into their office, which then must be built into a mutually beneficial relationship. This will result in more sales than any features/benefits data dump pitch could ever generate. But always remember to never take a "no" from someone who does not have the power to say "yes"!
– Michael C. Finegold, CEO/Global Sales Training Manager, Finegold & Associates

Buyer Expectation 3: Be More Professional

Historically, the roles of the salesperson and sales manager have focused on monthly or quarterly targets and results. Many sales professionals are forced into a commodity-selling environment that is transactional rather than strategic or consultative. However, in today's competitive landscape, sales professionals must focus on maintaining professionalism with buyers who may not have the same timeframe in mind or who may have strong negotiating skills. Salespeople must stay focused on delivering value to the buyer based on the buyer's goals and objectives, and can feel challenged by the need to balance revenue implications with ethical considerations. Keep in mind that successful sales professionals manage this fine balancing act while enduring the pressure to meet short-term quota attainment or new revenue goals.

Buyer Expectation 4: Listen More

To help buyers solve business problems, salespeople must have a strong understanding of the buyer's business, industry, customers, competitors, and products. The way to gain this knowledge is to *listen!* Today's successful sales professionals must be particularly skilled in listening, analyzing, problem solving, and questioning—perhaps even more so than possessing strong product knowledge. These skills enable salespeople to serve as trusted advisors by helping buyers navigate the complexity of the solution and the volume of available information. While communication skills are essential to success in any occupation, listening skills can help sellers identify root problems and hidden obstacles that could affect the buyer's business success. Listening also requires skill in building rapport, patience, and timing in order to build the foundation for a trusting relationship. As a result, listening provides the foundation for learning about problems and supplying relevant solutions.

STEP 4

POINTER

Always understand how your customer perceives you. You want to become their partner, not just someone who sells them something. If you keep in mind their role at their company and are able to find ways, with your product or service, to make them look great in their job role, you will have succeeded in becoming someone they can turn to again and again as easily as they would a coworker—a partner. At that point you will have achieved success.
– Renea Cox, Sales Consultant, Renea Cox

Buyer Expectation 5: For Buyers to Be Productive, Sellers Have to Be Productive

Traditionally, sales organizations have focused on volume of individual activity—number of calls made, number of presentations given—

as an indicator of productivity. Compensation was determined by meeting or exceeding sales quotas. Now, firms are instituting new metrics, such as profitability and customer service satisfaction. The relevance of a salesperson's activities can be scored and measured in addition to, or instead of, their frequency. These more sophisticated measures are surfacing as organizations attempt to shift or replace direct selling with lower-cost sales channels, such as telemarketing, direct mail, or email marketing. Plus, organizations must ensure that their sales team stays focused on the most appropriate use of time.

How to Define Value

How do buyers justify any purchase? One word—*value.* While all people define value differently, typically buyers define value in terms of wanting to increase personal security, increase professional status, make or save money, or gain more personal time.

These can be defined as

- **Security**—feeling secure or safety reasons
- **Time**—saving time, becoming more efficient, productivity, easier, provides a way to have more time off
- **Recognition**—looking good, keeping up with the competition, winning something
- **Money**—save money, make more money.

A *value proposition* is a clear statement of the tangible results a customer gets from using your products or services. The more specific your value proposition, the better. When you share a weak value proposition, clients think "so what?" and you've missed an opportunity to set your products and services apart from the competition. The value proposition you share with customers needs to include the WIIFM (what's in it for me) from their perspective.

Articulating a strong value proposition can deliver tangible results such as

- increased revenues
- faster time to market
- decreased costs

- improved operational efficiency
- increased market share
- decreased employee turnover
- improved customer retention levels.

A value proposition should *not* be based on features or benefits. It should be based on how you, your company, and your product or service can increase value. In communicating a value proposition to a prospective customer, focus on the three elements of a powerful sales message:

- **Feature**—what it is
- **Benefit**—what it does (for this specific audience)
- **Value**—what it's actually worth.

STEP 4

A *feature* is a specific aspect of a product or service. Every product or service offering can have multiple features. In fact, for many offerings, major features can be made up of multiple "sub" features. To what level of granularity do you need to be able to speak? The answer to that question can be found in this sales fact: *Nobody buys your product. They buy the product of your product.*

A *benefit* is what the feature actually does for the prospective customer. For example, "sleep mode" is a feature on many computers. What is the benefit of this feature? It allows a computer to go into a powered down mode without actually turning off.

A *value* is what the benefit of a feature is worth to the prospective customer. For example, a value of sleep mode is that it will decrease the amount of time it takes to get back to work once you choose to power the computer back up.

Each feature can provide multiple benefits. Each of the benefits you define may address one or more of the motivators that influence your prospective customer to consider making a purchase. These motivators are actually how your prospective customer defines value. Therefore, a value is what the benefit of a feature is worth to the prospective customer, as translated into security, time, recognition, or money.

Just as every product can have multiple features, and every feature can have multiple benefits, each benefit can offer many values. Multiple features can deliver on the same core value proposition. For example, another value of sleep mode on a computer is that it will save on electricity over an extended period of time (a money appeal). Another value of this feature is that you could use it when you prepare for a presentation. The laptop is ready with just a click of a button so that you avoid delays or having people feel uncomfortable if they might have had to otherwise wait for you to start the computer from a fully powered down state (recognition appeal).

Getting to Know the Buyer

When you sell a solution, you can either sell to the broad market or you can tailor the product to the specific needs of a particular buyer. Usually the marketing department creates a value proposition for the target market as a whole. The sales professional must then take that message and target it specifically onto one buyer who has unique needs, goals, and objectives.

Buyer knowledge makes you and your solution more relevant for each individual buyer, the organization, and the environment. Collectively, that knowledge can be "rolled up" into a snapshot of what you know about the buyer to help identify, manage, and close more sales.

Knowledge is power. The better you know the buyer, the smoother the transaction. By knowing the buyers, their motives, their interests, and their backgrounds, the better equipped you are to make informed decisions about whether they are the right people to sell to. During negotiations, knowing the buyers helps to resolve issues early in the process. The more you know about why the buyer wants to buy your solution, the better position you are in to know when to be firm in the negotiation and when to be flexible.

Walk in the Buyer's Shoes

Think about the last time you bought something complex or complicated. Have you ever bought a house or a car? If you have, I want you to think about that experience. Pause for a moment and reflect on your role, goal, and objective as the buyer of the house or car.

For example, if you have ever bought a car:

- How long did you spend thinking about the car model, color, and manufacturer before you purchased the car?
- How did you specifically choose to arrive at the location for your purchase? Did you end up at a dealership? If so, what choices did you make that led you there?
- How did you arrive to the actual decision? Whose advice did you heed? When did you say, "That is the one"? How much research did you do before making that purchase? What resources did you reference? Who did you talk to?
- More important, think about how long you owned that car. Was the experience over for you when you drove it home? Did you continue to evaluate your choice long after you signed the paperwork and drove it home?

You probably had a lot of choices to make regarding your purchase. Each of those choices represents your own personalized approach to making a purchase decision. That purchase decision may have taken a short time (half a day) or it may have taken a longer time (a few months). Either way, you had to progress from an initial need, through a definition of what you wanted and needed, to a negotiation phase with the seller, to an actual purchase, and then to an evaluation phase in which you determined how well your final decision met your initial need.

Remember the decisions you made that led to your final purchase decision. It was a series of steps you had to progress though in order to finalize your purchase. Realize that all people go through the same steps in the buying process; however, they all make their decisions differently.

How you sell should ultimately synchronize to how the buyer (or buying team) is making their purchase decisions. Do not assume they make their decisions in the same way. People on the same team of buyers can make their own unique decisions—and all of those buying decisions can be completely different than the decisions you make.

How Prospects and Clients Buy

You have to be realistic. If you cannot see how your solution will benefit the buyer *through the eyes of the buyer,* you will have less chance of closing the sale. Approach each sale with agility and flexibility in mind, knowing that a potential buyer has their own unique decision-making process.

When potential problem areas arise, it is best to address them early and overcome them in a positive way. That means you have to be in sync with the buyer, and you need to build an open and honest dialogue.

Knowledge of your buyers and their decision-making criteria can help you stay in sync and avoid wasting time in a situation where they are not serious about buying. The fact is, a buyer may indicate a great deal of interest but when it gets down to the wire, he or she may back out of the deal. Some buyers want to buy only on their terms and conditions, some may have too many decision makers to please, and others only want to buy the "perfect"

POINTER

Decision makers are often reassessing every spending and investment decision they make. They are looking for ways to reduce, delay, or cancel purchases and investment decisions and they are seeking certainty that desired results will be achieved as planned. Maintaining a relationship-focused sales approach will not cut much sway or add relevant value to buyers with a "spend less, delay, or cancel" mindset. To succeed in helping today's buying decision makers, you must move your style to a results-focused approach.
– Himanshu Deshmukh, Global Presales Consultant, Satyam Computers Services Ltd. (Tech Mahindra Co).

business. Wasting time on those who aren't serious about purchasing your solution takes valuable time away from those buyers who are ready to buy.

Another key piece of wisdom that sales professionals need to embrace is when to try and close the sale or not—meaning, is the client ready to buy yet. For example, perhaps a client or prospect exhibits the telltale buying signs:

- A client or prospect slows the pace of discussions as he or she makes a final analysis and decision of what to buy.
- The client or prospect has a tight deadline and increases the pace to move things along quicker or begins to engage procurement in the discussions.
- The client or prospect asks more and more detailed questions and/or tries to negotiate specific aspects of a business deal.

STEP 4

At times, though, these signs may be confusing. These signs could be part of the buying cycle. The buying cycle model describes a set of distinct phases that a prospect or client experiences when making buying decisions. Each of the steps in the process represents a series of decisions. Each of these decisions requires thought and strategy of a potential buyer and the buying organization. It is important for you to understand this buying cycle because it will unlock many mysteries about what is happening during the sales process. Remember, each decision along the way can be unique to each buyer. And more important, the buyer may make decisions that don't exactly match the decision that you would make if you were in his or her shoes.

To illustrate, Figure 4.1 depicts the buying cycle. Imagine a client needing to procure a product or service and the phases they experience in making the buying decision throughout the process. In particular, a client generally progresses through the following nine phases:

1. **Plan**—The buying organization outlines a plan for its business, such as its strategic plan, realignment of the organization, or the acquisition of new capabilities, or defines a new vision.

FIGURE 4.1

The Buying Cycle

Corporate Buying Strategy

B1	B2	B3	B4	B5	B6	B7	B8	B9
Plan	Recognize	Search	Assess	Choose	Obligate	Implement	Track	Integrate

Transaction Experience

STEP 4

2. **Recognize**—The buying organization realizes they have a need (based on what happened in phase 1) and seeks to satisfy that need. They begin to take action toward buying (as opposed to making their own solution or product). They act accordingly by setting forth goals, objectives, targets, and budgets. They may appoint a team of people to evaluate potential vendors in this phase.
3. **Search**—The buying organization engages in activities to find a vendor, partner, or supplier. They begin reviewing capabilities of selling organization(s) to see which one can meet their needs and with whom they would like to have a relationship.
4. **Assess**—The buying organization requests proposals, conducts more in-depth meetings, requests more detailed information, has more serious dialogue, and conducts an analysis of risk. The buying organization mitigates risk as much as possible.
5. **Choose**—The buying organization has narrowed the choices down to one organization and begins "testing the

water" to gauge the organization's ability of fulfillment. If the benefits outweigh risks, the buying organization begins talking about implementation.

6. **Obligate**—The buying organization writes the check or signs the proposal. Key decision makers have put their reputations on the line. Their decisions, and the money they have set aside, will move the entire affected organization in a new direction.
7. **Implement**—The buying organization is now a customer or client and begins implementing the selected solution. They realign organizational resources as necessary, and put long-term plans together.
8. **Track**—The customer formally or informally begins documenting the selling organization's ability to fulfill the solution. The buying organization looks for a return on their investment and justification to further or continue the relationship.
9. **Integrate**—The buying organization integrates the product or service into the competencies necessary to create their own products or services, and begins to obtain maximum use of the product or service from within.

Instead of focusing internally and only on the selling organization (like traditional sales funnels facilitate), the buying cycle helps you remain focused on the entire customer experience—even after the sale. The more effective you become at understanding what the buyer does, the more you will sell. This is extremely important because in today's business world, buyers are much more knowledgeable of the choices they have.

POINTER

Poker champions know that it's not what's in your hand that counts, but what's in the other guy's hand. With selling, it's not your product that counts, but the customer's needs and requirements. Quit playing your hand; play their needs.
– Dave Millman, Vice President Marketing, Ciranova, Inc.

Obviously, the goal of selling is to have the customer attain a return-on-investment (ROI) in pre- and post-sales processes, and return-on-assets (ROA) once the purchase is capitalized. Ideally, the product or service will become fully integrated, leveraged, and justified. From a relationship perspective, the buying and selling organizations begin to work with a more trust-based bond.

For a transaction to occur, the buying organization must progress through every phase of the buying cycle; however, the length of time spent in each phase may be slowed or accelerated, and a buyer may also exit the cycle at any time, for any reason.

The nine phases may occur over an hour or they may take years. Whatever the length of the buying cycle in the organization or whatever the product or service being evaluated, the buying organization is always in one of these nine phases. When a buying decision is made, it results in a decision to "buy" or "not buy." This is often referred to as closing or losing the sale. Obviously, sales professionals would like to close the most deals as possible to bring in greater revenue for their companies.

STEP 4

If the buyer decides to purchase, then the seller and the seller's organization are obligated to provide the product or service within the terms and conditions of the documentation necessary to fulfill the order. If the seller decides not to buy, then hopefully that decision was due to a poor fit between the buyer's need and the seller's solution. No matter what, it should be a win–win decision.

Some phases are more important at different times. For instance, a company deciding whether or not to purchase a highly complex solution would place more emphasis on the choosing phase (phase 5) to ensure a smooth implementation in later phases.

Who Makes and Influences the Buying Decision?

Just as no two people are alike, not all buyers act the same way. Throughout the buying cycle, myriad key players may be involved in the buying decision. The most successful sales professionals correctly identify the individual motivations and roles these buyers play in the process.

- The *executive signer* is the person who actually makes the purchase and ultimately and acts as a final decision maker.
- The *initiator* is the person who first suggests or thinks of the idea to buy a product or service.
- The *coach* is the person who helps the selling organization determine the parts of the buying decision. The coach may help the selling organization identify whether or not the buying organization will buy, what they intend to buy, how they buy, when they will buy, or even where they will buy from.
- The *influencer* is the person who explicitly or implicitly carries some influence over the final decision.
- The *requirements decision maker* evaluates based on practical realities of adding a selling organization's product or service offering to day-to-day processes of the company.
- The *financial decision maker* evaluates and recommends based on costs, budgets, and return-on-investment.
- The *end-user* is the person or people who consume or use the product or service. They will use your product or service every day.

STEP 4

Regardless of the type of buyer and his or her motivations, it's no secret that gaining and keeping long-term clients is dependent on a sales professional's ability to build trust and credibility.

Understanding Negotiation Strategies

As a salesperson, you often deal with "C-level" executives (CEO, CFO, CMO, and so on). These individuals have most likely been trained in negotiation strategies, and it is important for you to be aware of these tactics.

There are several strategies you can employ when negotiating with a buyer. These strategies are based on the perception they have about the outcome. Perception is an important word, because perception is reality in selling. For example, a "win" results when the outcome of a negotiation is better than expected; a "loss" when the outcome is worse than expected. The win or loss could be perceived differently by the buyer and the seller (you).

For example, you and the buyer may receive the same outcome in measurable terms, say the buyer purchased products or services for $10,000. However, for the seller (you) that may be a loss if the total implementation or service fees were calculated to be worth more than $10,000. In this same situation, this could be a win for the buyer if the buyer received more value than what he or she paid. In other words, it's the expectations of the buyer and seller that determine the result of the negotiation.

From the seller's (your) perspective, there are three different ways to view the negotiation:

- **Win–win strategies**—A win–win outcome occurs when each side of the negotiation perceives that they have won. Since both sides benefit from such a scenario, any resolutions to the negotiation are likely to be accepted voluntarily. Ideally, the negotiation process aims to achieve win–win outcomes.
- **Win–lose strategies**—A win–lose outcome occurs when only one side perceives the negotiation outcome as positive. Thus, win–lose negotiations are less likely to be accepted voluntarily. Bargaining processes that are based on a high degree of competition between participants tend to end in win–lose outcomes.
- **Lose–lose strategies**—A lose–lose outcome occurs when both the buyer and the seller (you) perceive a loss. An example of this would be a budget-cutting negotiation in which all parties lose money. In some lose–lose situations, all parties understand that losses are unavoidable and that they will be even. In such situations, lose–lose outcomes can be preferable to win–lose outcomes because the distribution is at least considered to be fair.

The key thing to remember is that any negotiation strategy may be changed or can be influenced to change.

Knowledge of these strategies can help you understand when to walk away from a deal. Too many sellers get so involved in trying to put a deal together that they don't see the big picture. They don't realize that the deal isn't a good one. Many salespeople don't want to let the deal get away. Since they have invested a lot of time and effort, and probably expenses, it's often difficult to just end it. However, in some cases, that's exactly what must be done. If the deal isn't right, and can't be fixed, there is no other choice. It's much better not to do a deal than to do a bad one.

Understanding how clients buy services can make or break your sales pipeline. It isn't enough to know how to market and sell; you have to understand how your clients buy. This step reviewed the buying process, how customers define value, who influences buying decisions, and suggestions for negotiating strategies. Now that you have an understanding of client considerations during the buying process, the next step is to master key information about the selling process.

WORKSHEET 4.1

Sharing Best Practices

Instructions: Now that you know the nine phases of the buying cycle, you need to think about what it takes to help facilitate buyer decision making. This worksheet will help you identify actions, tools, and resources you need to have for each step in the cycle. More important, you will be able to identify what questions you may have for your manager or colleagues to help you share best practices. You can refer to the definition of each buying cycle phase from earlier in this step as you fill out the information below.

Once you have filled it out, you can begin to map your sales process to these phases. Remember that each buyer will have his or her own unique decision-making criteria for each phase. Take into consideration the multiple decision makers you may encounter. To help, think of a specific deal you are working now.

Steps	Actions, Tools, and Resources I Need
1. Plan	
Buyer(s) need in this step	
Actions I need to take in this step	
Tools and resources I need in this step	
Questions I have for my manager or colleagues	
Best practices I identified	
2. Recognize	
Buyer(s) need in this step	
Actions I need to take in this step	
Tools and resources I need in this step	
Questions I have for my manager or colleagues	
Best practices I identified	

continued on next page

Worksheet 4.1, continued

Steps	Actions, Tools, and Resources I Need
3. Search	
Buyer(s) need in this step	
Actions I need to take in this step	
Tools and resources I need in this step	
Questions I have for my manager or colleagues	
Best practices I identified	
4. Assess	
Buyer(s) need in this step	
Actions I need to take in this step	
Tools and resources I need in this step	
Questions I have for my manager or colleagues	
Best practices I identified	
5. Choose	
Buyer(s) need in this step	
Actions I need to take in this step	
Tools and resources I need in this step	
Questions I have for my manager or colleagues	
Best practices I identified	

Worksheet 4.1, continued

Steps	Actions, Tools, and Resources I Need
6. Obligate	
Buyer(s) need in this step	
Actions I need to take in this step	
Tools and resources I need in this step	
Questions I have for my manager or colleagues	
Best practices I identified	
7. Implement	
Buyer(s) need in this step	
Actions I need to take in this step	
Tools and resources I need in this step	
Questions I have for my manager or colleagues	
Best practices I identified	
8. Track	
Buyer(s) need in this step	
Actions I need to take in this step	
Tools and resources I need in this step	
Questions I have for my manager or colleagues	
Best practices I identified	

continued on next page

Worksheet 4.1, continued

Steps	Actions, Tools, and Resources I Need
9. Integrate	
Buyer(s) need in this step	
Actions I need to take in this step	
Tools and resources I need in this step	
Questions I have for my manager or colleagues	
Best practices I identified	

STEP 4

STEP FIVE

Leverage the Sales Process

OVERVIEW

- Prospecting
- Approaching and qualifying
- Presenting and discovering
- Committing
- Following up

The sales process is one of many processes that play an important role in your toolkit. All professional salespeople should follow a sales process they have internalized and call their own. Why? Because most sales professionals recognize the sales process exists, but they have tailored it to meet their own personal needs. They don't just accept a taught sales process at face value. They build their own personal selling system by taking a piece of knowledge from a sales training class, another piece of knowledge from a book, and another piece of knowledge from a colleague. The importance of this process is that it helps you

- organize your day
- organize customer knowledge
- have a common language and structure
- measure success
- diagnose procedural or policy challenges
- create a personalized selling system.

While all salespeople are aware of the sales process, very few have internalized it to the point where they can recite it from memory.

- Should you follow a sales process? Yes.
- Should you learn a sales process? Yes.
- Should you customize a sales process that works for you? Yes.
- Do all customers fit within a nicely packaged sales process all the time? No.
- Are all buying processes linear and step by step? No.

POINTER

One often-overlooked sales best practice is the importance of aligning your solution to the customer's business issues. Too often salespeople are simply selling the features and benefits of their product without truly understanding the industry of their customer. It's important, especially if you're selling in a vertical market like healthcare, banking, IT, or something else to know the trends impacting your potential customer. Then ask yourself, what problems and consequences will this company experience if they don't have my solution? Once that is understood, begin asking questions that get the customer to acknowledge the problems and consequences exist.
– Steve Gielda, Principal, Sales Momentum

You can read books and attend seminars and training on sales processes; there are literally hundreds of rebranded, repackaged, and re-taught sales processes available to you. All of them are technically "correct." There isn't one "best sales process" for you to follow.

Since most sales processes follow seven steps that have existed since the early 1900s, you should gain an understanding of the typical 7-step sales process in Figure 5.1. Understanding and internalizing the process will help you build a foundation for a successful career by getting you off to a quick start in understanding where the buyer is in their decision making and helping you "sort" the information, knowledge, and environmental inputs you'll receive on a minute-by-minute basis. The key to internalizing the sales process is to learn and apply the process in an appropriate manner that synchronizes to the buyer while retaining flexibility and adaptability. This process, while appearing to be

FIGURE 5.1

A Typical 7-Step Selling Process

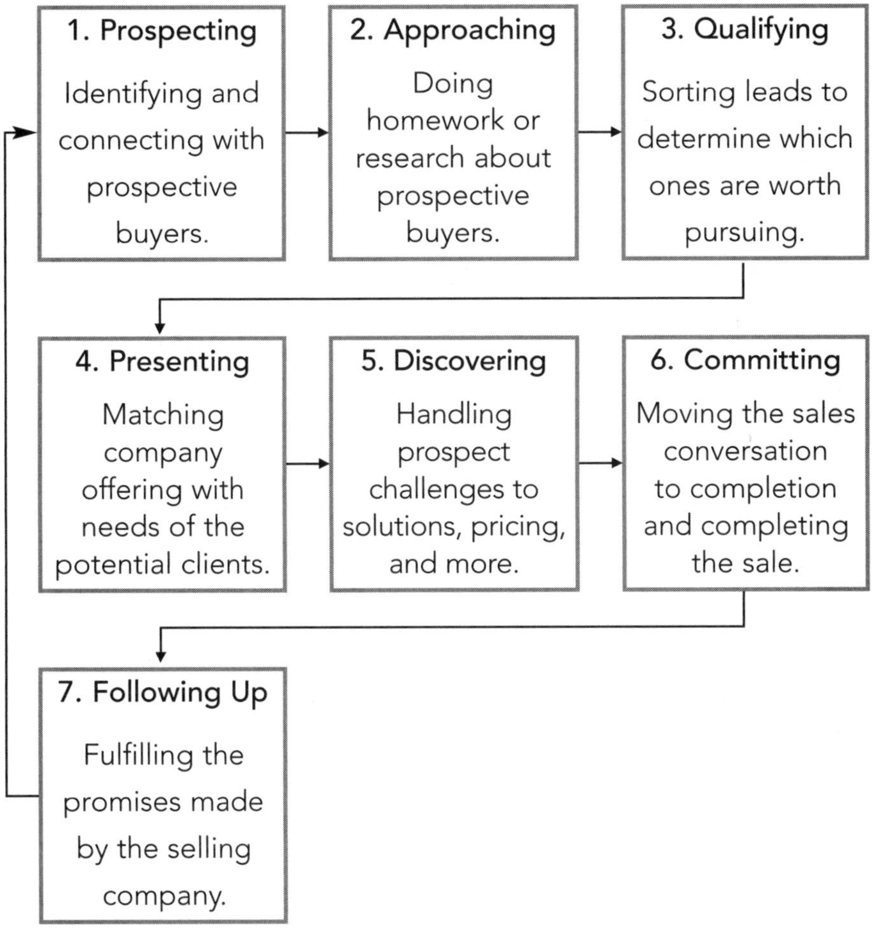
1. Prospecting
Identifying and connecting with prospective buyers.
2. Approaching
Doing homework or research about prospective buyers.
3. Qualifying
Sorting leads to determine which ones are worth pursuing.
4. Presenting
Matching company offering with needs of the potential clients.
5. Discovering
Handling prospect challenges to solutions, pricing, and more.
6. Committing
Moving the sales conversation to completion and completing the sale.
7. Following Up
Fulfilling the promises made by the selling company.

linear, in reality loops back on itself, allows for multiple points of entry, and helps you harness the chaos of professional selling. In fact, when you fold in marketing processes, planning processes, communication processes, and other important selling processes, the sales process that I outline below will serve only as starting point to keeping you organized as you build multiple relationships to become a trusted advisor.

Creativity within the sales process is important because most buyers have been taught the 7-step sales process and so have most other salespeople (including your competition). To begin, focus on understanding the 7-step selling process to build a solid foundation, including what each phase involves, possible outputs and results you need to achieve, and suggested ways for you to learn and master each step.

Step 1: Prospecting

- **Definition**—Prospecting is the ability to identify and connect with potential customers. In some organizations, the company invests money in advertising and turns these prospected leads over to you. However, many firms expect you to find these prospects and initiate a sales dialogue.
- **What You Need to Know and Do**
  - Utilize sales and marketing collateral resources.
  - Display effective cold-calling techniques.
  - Possess customer-related vertical market or industry knowledge.
  - Display business alliance building skills.
  - Effectively lead meetings and facilitate discussions.
  - Display effective people management skills.
  - Know competitive information resources.
  - Actively use trust-building and selling techniques.
  - Leverage marketing programs to advance sales.
  - Translate competitive knowledge into relevant sales practices.
- **Possible Outputs**—Creating a list of locations where you can connect with potential clients. Joining appropriate associations or groups, attending activities, or calling on the resources you have identified in this step. You need to learn to be sensitive to the time invested in finding prospects. Joining associations and attending tradeshows

should be scrutinized, even quantified, to determine their value as resources to land new business.

- **Suggested Ways to Learn**—Brainstorming with other sales professionals and management on how to find prospects and provide information about organizations, meetings, and tradeshows where prospects gather.

Step 2: Approaching

- **Definition**—The approaching step is the homework, or research, phase of the selling process. It is essential and easy for a professional to gather data on a company and even details on the specific prospect. Preparing this information prior to initiating a conversation arms a salesperson with details that help paint a broad picture about the prospect's company, its role in its industry, and more. This effort positions the salesperson as a professional who understands as much as possible about the environment he or she will encounter when selling to this firm.

> **POINTER**
>
> Don't memorize a pitch—learn your product well and simply have a conversation about it. It will be more natural and feel less rehearsed.
> *– Travis L. Ford, Marketing Specialist, KBAK TV-29 (CBS)/KBFX TV-58 (FOX)*

STEP 5

- **What You Need to Know and Do**
  - Utilize formal and ad hoc research strategies (for example, systematic exploration, personal networking, website scanning).
  - Be aware of internal resources (technical, pricing, legal, delivery and fulfillment).
  - Use industry research engines and resources (for example, Dun and Bradstreet, analyst reports).
  - Determine appropriate customer organizational communication resources (websites, blogs, annual reports, press releases, position and white papers).
  - Calculate business health indictors (for example, ratios).

- Explain solution configuration frameworks or templates.
- Observe differences in the business environment for technical solution definition.
- Design specific vertical industry solutions based on industry needs.
- Interpret and synthesize information from multiple sources.
- Distinguish well-targeted sales messages from generic messages.
- Apply relevant account planning tools, templates, and procedures.
- Apply funnel management practices, tools, metrics, and policies effectively to prioritize and manage selling.
- Manage technical teams and integrate their contributions.

- **Possible Outputs**—Acquire knowledge and insights into the company and the prospect. Be able to contact and establish a dialogue and relationship. Collect information from databases and reference sources online or in print form. Become familiar with these resources so you can find them quickly. Plan time to do pre-approach research (it should not be during prime selling time).
- **Suggested Ways to Learn**—Listen to a sales training session online. Attend sales training. View a demonstration of web and company resources for researching.

Step 3: Qualifying

- **Definition**—Qualifying involves sorting through leads to find the ones that are worthy of your time and attention. Chasing poor prospects is a serious problem with most sales organizations, and you need to be realistic in your investment of time with potential customers. This qualification process can occur prior to engaging prospects (through print or online methods), or it can be used in initial conversations with prospects to identify whether to pursue the relationship further.

- **What You Need to Know and Do**
  - Administer lead management procedures.
  - Calculate cost estimates and sizing techniques.
  - Qualify opportunities.
  - Know the customer's business and operations (for example, reporting structures, decision makers).
  - Test various business analysis methods.
  - Manage the sales process tools, metrics, and policies.
  - Utilize resource management strategies.
  - Analyze and manage requirements.
  - Effectively size solutions for scope and impact.
  - Leverage vertical market and industry knowledge in product or service positioning.
  - Utilize business and social networking sites where appropriate.
  - Lead business analysis discussions.
  - Determine how customers are organized and how they make purchasing decisions.
  - Summarize salient content from customer communication sources.
  - Determine business health and viability using key business ratios.
  - Map customer's product or service operating environment.

> **POINTER**
> If you are selling an exceptional product, one does not have to be exceptional at selling it.
> – *Raoul G. Dexters, Marketing Director, International Biscuits & Confections*

- **Possible Outputs**—Establish criteria, perhaps five or six items, based on what your company or management deems great potential customers. You should be able to identify the exact criteria of a great prospect, and provide an analysis of existing best customers to define and produce a list of qualifying questions based on those criteria. You also should be able to use questioning skills to discover whether money is set aside for the purchase, a current need to buy exists, the proper decision maker is the contact, and so forth. Know when to walk away from those that don't fit specific criteria. Simply put, the best reps spend more time with the best prospects.

- **Suggested Ways to Learn**—Brainstorm and/or model elevator speeches, role-play opening dialogues with prospects, have group discussions, participate in question-and-answer sessions to identify great prospects versus poor ones, and view video or live simulations of good and bad prospects so you can distinguish the difference. Put together a list of criteria and craft questions that help you identify whether the prospect is qualified. Keep this document handy until these questions become part of your normal buyer–seller conversations.

Step 4: Presenting

- **Definition**—The presenting step is defined by a commitment of both parties to have a dialogue to determine if the selling company can best serve the buying company and whether further steps need to be taken. It is an opportunity for you to begin deepening the relationship by attempting to match your company's offerings to the needs of the prospect. However, this is where most sales reps begin to encounter resistance and is the most complex part of any sales process.
- **What You Need to Know and Do**
  - Demonstrate personal engagement and interest-generation strategies.
  - Calculate business analysis metrics (health ratios, balance sheet analysis).
  - Describe the supply chain (lead times, response rates, fulfillment processes).
  - Differentiate product/service/solution technology (concepts, uses).
  - Break down solution technical foundations.

- Select solution design procedures and communication conventions (written or graphical).
- Explain solution design methodologies, best practices, and trends.
- Experiment with oral and written communication skills to determine the most effective.

POINTER

Keep calling, and never take "no" personally. Anyone who tells you that you don't have to cold call is lying.
– Robert Minskoff, Freelance Sales Consultant, Salesman4Hire

- Display professional customer-facing skills.
- Lead technical teams.
- Adapt listening skills appropriately.
- Create compelling sales presentations.
- Communicate product or service benefits and features in a compelling manner.
- Communicate features and benefits of solution-related tools or packages.
- Justify technical solutions.

◆ **Possible Outputs**—You should be able to craft a presentation that effectively delivers the value proposition. You must quickly get to the point by asking questions in order to determine how to best present your solution to the prospect. In essence, you must have the ability to adapt and change direction in a conversation to match the buyer's interests while advancing the sale toward the close. You should also be able to set boundaries on the time allowed for the presentation to help you keep focus and respect the buyer's time.

◆ **Suggested Ways to Learn**—Participate in video or live demonstrations of a sample presentation. Take part in a group discussion and brainstorming to craft the best language to present the company and its offerings. Participate in role-plays to simulate buyer–seller encounters. Ride along with (or listen to) high-performing colleagues in order to observe successful behavior.

Step 5: Discovering

- **Definition**—This step is where the selling process can get quite intense—prospects challenge solutions, pricing, and more. Your ability to build value for the client and handle resistance is often one of the truest measures of your ability to succeed as a sales professional. Typically, most salespeople might encounter five or six questions (or more) regarding a product or service offering. While many people might call these "objections," the important part of this step involves discovering what other information your prospective customer needs in order to make a decision. If you do your job right, you won't need to "overcome objections" at all. This step is an important qualitative measure of sales success, particularly with new sales reps.
- **What You Need to Know and Do**
  - Sales negotiation and closing methods.
  - Return-on-investment (ROI) and total cost of ownership (TCO) techniques.
  - Objection-handling techniques.
  - Estimates of cost and appropriate size of solutions.
  - Calculate business metrics and translate product or service features into value propositions.
  - Counter-propose competitor product or service feature and benefit messages.
  - Translate solution designs into meaningful customer benefits, and differentiate these by stakeholder needs.
- **Possible Outputs**—Recognize and respond to the top half-dozen objections or standard questions you encounter in prospect interactions. You should be able to think of three or more responses to each objection. In role-playing, these responses should be practiced in a relaxed, confident, and professional manner. Be careful not to get anxious or defensive when you meet resistance. This type of dialogue will erode goodwill and eliminate any progress made prior to this point in the sales process.

- **Suggested Ways to Learn**—Demonstration and role-play; brainstorm responses to objections; have question-and-answer sessions with experienced reps leading discussions; create documentation of objection responses for you to keep handy; ride along with (or listen to) others to observe successful behavior. Create a list of the top six objections with several responses for each that you are most comfortable using. Keep this document handy until these responses become part of your normal buyer–seller conversations.

> **POINTER**
>
> Don't be afraid of rejection—just embrace it.
>
> *– Rob Johnson, Executive Recruiter*

Step 6: Committing

- **Definition**—The commitment step is to selling what a finish line is to racing. This is the prize you have been working hard for. The committing phase is often called "closing," but if you think about it from the buyer's perspective, it's really the "opening" or beginning to the relationship. The key to reaching and surpassing this step is based on your ability to move the conversation forward to a logical conclusion, and then to know when to ask the buyer for commitment. Closing questions are phrases that can test the buyer's belief about working with the proposed solution. The language choices might vary from rep to rep. The time to ask might vary from buyer to buyer. But if the purpose of the selling relationship is to end it with a yes (a purchase) or a no (disqualified prospect), then this step gives you the ability to focus your actions and outputs.
- **What You Need to Know and Do**
  - Develop proposals, component integration, and management practices.
  - Predict negotiation positions and strategies.

- Utilize effective closing techniques.
- Transition from "hunting" to "farming" practices where appropriate (new business oriented versus selling to existing clients).
- Deploy practices and back-office administrative or order-entry procedures.
- Develop solutions.
- Manage expectations (expectation setting, quality checking).
- Determine buyer readiness from verbal and nonverbal cues.
- Manage multiple or interrelated sales calls.
- Manage leads and ensure follow-up or follow-through.
- Align sales actions to the current point within the sales process.
- Coordinate and align all activities with a solid plan for success.
- Set accurate customer expectations for order fulfillment.
- Ensure cost-effective solution deployment and delivery practices.

- **Possible Outputs**—Recognize when and how to ask the buyer to buy. Understand who else, besides the primary buyer, is really involved in the decision-making process. Know the difference between casual conversations and conversations that advance the process. You should appear focused at all times, and know when you are near the end of a conversation in which the prospect will buy. You should be able to articulate direct closing language.
- **Suggested Ways to Learn**—Participate in demonstrations and role-play; take part in group discussions to create lists of closing questions; ride along with highly successful colleagues in order to observe successful behavior. You should be practicing closing conversations alone and with others, so that the language you use comes across casually, but firmly with the buyer. This personalized closing language should be printed out so you can make it part of your natural conversations with buyers.

Step 7: Following Up

> **POINTER**
> Simply put, the best skill any seller can have is to understand how they like to be sold to themselves!
> *– Chris Norfolk, Head of Direct Sales, Intuit UK*

- **Definition**—The previous commitment step isn't the end of the game—following up is an important step, but it probably won't be your last. Following up involves fulfillment of the promises made by the selling company. Here is where the new customer is going to be delighted or disappointed with his or her decision. Following up well is essential to staying connected to customers. This helps you get high-quality and qualified referrals, and eliminates some of the earlier steps in the sales process. It's good to remember that the sale is not complete when the buyer signs an agreement; it is complete after the check clears the bank. However, the relationship isn't over until the buyer stops using your product or solution. Deep customer relationships are very satisfying to a sales rep who often encounters a great deal of rejection in the course of his or her selling life.
- **What You Need to Know**
  - Be knowledgeable about account history (prior investments, account relationships).
  - Choose appropriate account planning tools, templates, and procedures.
  - Prioritize account-related marketing plans.
  - Manage contract administration and renewal processes.
  - Differentiate and monitor contractual and service-level agreement (SLA) terms, conditions, and milestone metrics.
  - Manage total customer satisfaction to optimize relationships.
  - Leverage contract administration and renewal into up- or cross-selling opportunities.

    - Develop trusted advisor status with customers based on technical acumen.
- **Possible Outputs**—Learn to reconnect with the buyer after he or she has committed to purchase. Affirm his or her decision about buying, see that products and services are delivered as promised, and ask—when appropriate—for referrals. This last piece is about implementing a fulfillment process that gives the buyer what he or she bought. The company should determine exactly what this is prior to the sale's completion. Set a time at the "close" for a follow-up dialogue or meeting to reconnect with the buyer. Don't forget to request referrals from a new client! Establish the language that is most comfortable for you to ask for referrals.
- **Suggested Ways to Learn**—Attend sales training on the steps to complete a sale. Introduce yourself to support personnel. Make sure you know how to fill out forms and follow processes to complete order fulfillment and book revenue. Participate in brainstorming and group discussions on requesting referrals after the sale is complete. Gain enough knowledge of internal policies and procedures so you can ensure a smooth transition after the sale. You should also be able to coach others on how to get great referrals.

Understanding the buying process is only half of the equation. Understanding the selling process is also essential to managing the complexity of selling. Just remember that there are multiple processes working together in your work, and the sales process can be nonlinear and often chaotic. The next step builds on the selling process and focuses on how you can customize it to create your own selling system and unleash success.

WORKSHEET 5.1

Worksheet Pre-Call Planning

Instructions: In today's business world, customers have more choices than ever before, and more information is readily available that they can locate on their own to make informed decisions. In this environment, the most successful sales professionals add value in the sales process. Otherwise, customers will either go elsewhere or use price as the primary reason for buying.

When meeting with customers, many sales professionals often have just a few precious minutes of time in which to gather information and discuss their products. For this reason, it is critical that salespeople effectively pre-call plan before meeting with a client. This worksheet will help you to accomplish this goal and ensure that you know key information about the client and his or her company before your call.

Company Knowledge

Topic	Information
Name of Company	
Name of Primary Contact(s)	
Industry	
Last year's revenues and profits	
Stock performance over past 12–24 months	
Organizational structure	
Key people	
Number of employees	
Number of locations	
Key products	
Target markets	
Distribution mechanism	

continued on next page

STEP 5

Worksheet 5.1, continued

Topic	Information
Market share	
Marketing activities	
Short-term strategy	
Long-term strategy	
Key business issues	
Topic of recent articles or news releases	
Key customers	

STEP 5

Pre-Call Plan

Topic	Information
Name of Company	
Industry	
Name of Primary Contact(s)	
Date	
Purpose of this sales call	
Name and titles of attendees	
Where are they in their buying process (collectively and individually)?	
What specific actions do I want out of this conversation to advance the discussion?	

Worksheet 5.1, continued

Anticipated Current Business Challenges and Issues

Operations challenges/overview

Questions to ask

Marketing and sales challenges/overview

Questions to ask

Organization and management challenges/overview

Questions to ask

Recent company changes

Questions to ask

STEP 5

NOTES

STEP SIX

Create Your Personal Sales System

OVERVIEW

- Your personal sales system
- Identifying your sales mental model
- The sales funnel is dead!
- Your four-stage personal selling approach
- Increase your sales effectiveness

In Steps 1–3, you learned how to be an effective sales professional, and Steps 4–5 focused on how to be an efficient salesperson by understanding the buying process and leveraging the sales process. In Step 6, using the information in the first five steps, you can build your own unique, personalized, and tailored approach to professional selling.

To succeed in managing the complexity around you, you must be able to meet the buyer where they are in their buying process, make the right choices, and remain poised, calm, and professional. As Eric Kerkhoff, an account executive with Hewlett-Packard, said, "The sales profession is chaotic, complex, and constantly changing. What you do to manage the complexity around you really matters. More important, your ability to do so will set you apart as a trusted advisor who can really make a difference in the buyer(s) situation." But how can you create a personal sales system when each company you work for is unique, each buying organization you encounter has its own buying processes, and the buyer(s) within them all have different decision-making criteria?

The answer lies in understanding how to model your own personal sales system.

Model Your Personal Sales System

The Random House unabridged dictionary (2008) defines a system as

- an ordered and comprehensive assemblage of facts, principles, doctrines, or the like within a particular field of knowledge or thought.
- a combination of things or parts that form a complex or unitary whole.

A systems approach to professional selling is important because professional selling is a system—period. It's not an isolated event. It's not just about the buyer, and it's not just about a seller. It's also not just about market dynamics. It is about managing the sales chaos to become a trusted advisor. That means you have to approach it as a system.

STEP 6

Approaching the sales profession as a system allows you to accomplish two things. First, it allows you to look at what you do as an ever-changing and dynamic job function. This means you need to have the ability to look at what you do and what you know with an open mind. There are several approaches you can take that will help you to think of the components of your personal sales system in this fashion. Second, it allows you to experience freedom and control within an existing framework. The framework you create as your own personal sales system will then allow you to maintain control and manage the sales process, while at the same time allow you to be agile, flexible, and creative with clients.

Use Mental Models to Identify Your Personal Sales System

How do you approach professional selling? What's your mental model (or paradigm)? A mental model is an explanation of a thought process for how something works in the real world. It is a representation of the surrounding world, and the relationships between various parts. The mental model can also show you how you contribute to the organization through your work. For example, the way you approach professional selling can contribute to building customer trust—or not. If you don't approach professional selling as a system, your mental model will not be large enough to handle the complexity around you. Your perceptions and "gut feel" won't be easy to replicate, and you will not understand how the choices you make contributed to results you achieved.

In Figure 6.1, the mental model represents the scope and size of the professional selling system. The figure shows how your mental model defines your personal selling system. Your mental model and personal selling system ultimately shape environmental inputs to create customer trust through your work.

Based on years of real-world professional sales and sales training experience, the following mental models can

POINTER

Successful salespeople believe that hyper-communication breeds success by default. Pick up a phone, send a letter, write an email, fax a special, and visit with anticipated regularity. Build these activities into your schedule. The more informed every customer is regarding your own personal goals and how they drive you to support them, your company's underlying objectives, upcoming changes relating to products, services, processes, and personnel, and sincere reasons behind why they should take action on your recommendations, the more successful and relevant the representative will become. The reciprocal is also true. Know your customers as individuals with hopes, dreams, goals, likes, and dislikes as well, and not just a means to an end. People can enrich your life if you take the time to know them on a deeper level. Incremental versus organic lifts in productivity will ensue. You must keep the lines of communication flowing. Let your customers know that they are important to you as people and are appreciated well beyond the transactional level. Be top-of-mind with what matters most and your customers will cherish that personal relationship for many years to come.
– Michael S. Fredricks, Director of Sales, Expanded Channels, Culligan International

FIGURE 6.1

Sales Mental Model Process

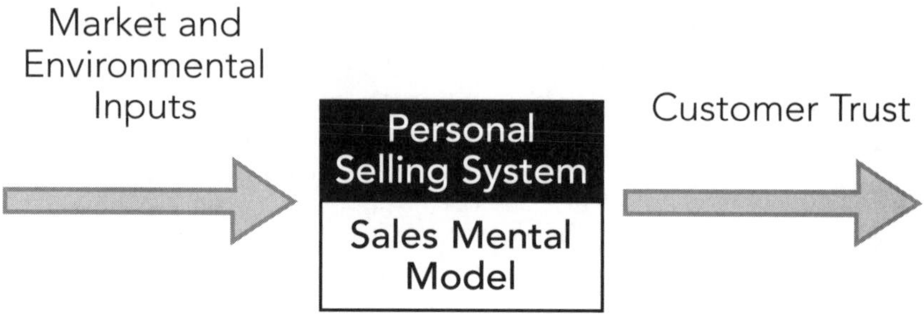

help you identify and craft your personal sales system in order to define your approach to solving problems and carrying out sales-related activities.

STEP 6

Sales Assembly Line Approach

With this mental model, view professional selling like an assembly line. To create the assembly line, break down buyer–seller relationships into compartmentalized processes or steps. Each step has an input and an output, as well as key measures of quality and success. With this approach, begin to "assemble the sale" with input from the buyer at the beginning of the process. This allows you to isolate the sales function and make sure it's running smoothly. A sale "comes off the assembly line" when the deal is closed.

> **POINTER**
>
> Remember that you cannot create demand from nothing. You must define demand. Companies that think they can create demand from scratch are living a dream. They can only create solutions that meet a specific need in the marketplace.
> *– Eric Kerkhoff, Account Executive, Hewlett-Packard Company*

Much like an automobile assembly line, each part of the sales assembly

FIGURE 6.2

Sales Assembly Line Mental Model

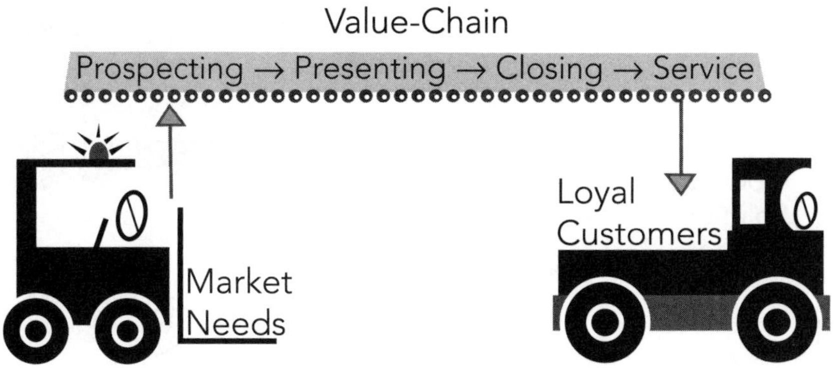

line can be improved and streamlined with new people, processes, or technology. This mental model focuses on continuous improvement and zero defects within the sales process. As a result, this mental model helps you manage your efficiency and assumes that buyers buy in a linear fashion. Be careful with this approach because the buyer is easily forgotten, isolated, or misrepresented. This mental model is how most salespeople view professional selling.

STEP 6

Sales Manufacturing Plant Approach

With this mental model, the assembly line model sits within the larger "sales manufacturing plant." Much like an automobile manufacturing plant, sales information can be warehoused, knowledge can be shuffled around, and the solution can be packed up for delivery within the manufacturing plant mental model.

> **POINTER**
>
> People buy from people they trust and like!
>
> *– Maria A. Ruggieri, Assistant Manager, Sales Consultant, American Laser Center*

FIGURE 6.3

Sales Manufacturing Plant Mental Model

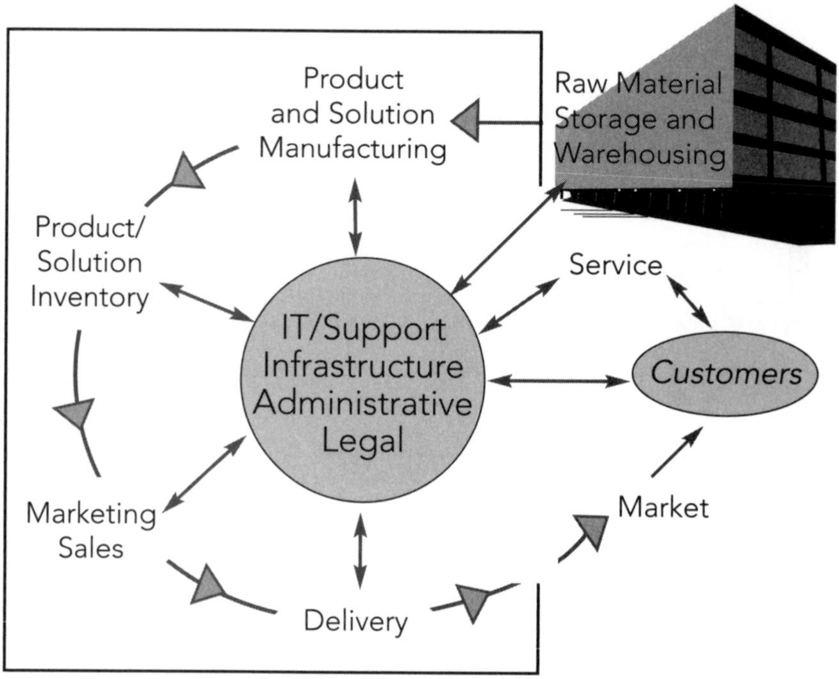

STEP 6

More important, the sales function can be viewed all the way from lead generation and marketing through the close. While the sales assembly line mental model focuses on the sales process, the manufacturing plan mental model allows you to look at the key linkages between

- selling and management
- selling and marketing
- selling and service
- selling and infrastructure (IT)
- selling and back-office support
- selling and legal, and so on.

Helicopter Approach

This mental model allows you to remove yourself from the professional selling environment and get above the fray. To do this, visualize yourself in a helicopter hovering above the buyer–seller relationship. The higher up you go, the more area you see, but with less focus on each specific area.

"Hovering in the helicopter" at the lowest level allows you to view the sales department from above. At this level you look down and see all the moving parts of your sales and marketing organization. These parts work together to help you sell (at least they're supposed to). By hovering at this level, you can see the processes, outputs, and strategies employed by your sales colleagues, sales management, and marketing team.

The next level up allows you to isolate the relationship you have with one customer. Now, not only is your organization in view

FIGURE 6.4

Helicopter Approach Mental Model

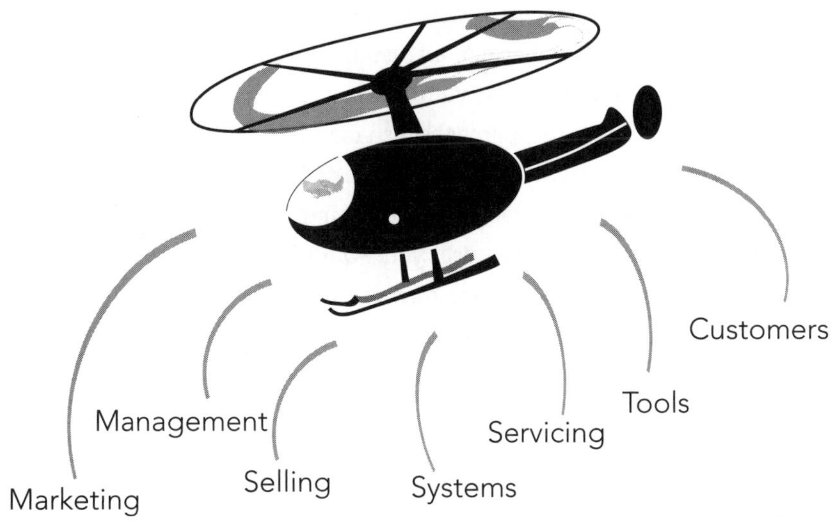

POINTER

I began my career selling door-to-door and saw a ton of rejection. I tell new salespeople to practice genuinely smiling everyday wherever you go. Your mere presence will emit a very warm, calm, and inviting vibe. This one action alone motivates people to want to meet you and hear your message.
– Mike Bondi, Business Networking Facilitator, Networking Success Group

but the buying organization should come into focus. At this level, you will be able to see the buying processes, buying outputs, and buying strategies that your customer employs.

At the next level, you see your entire sales portfolio. The individual sales organization will lose some focus; however, you'll be able to see more of the market forces at work. You will be able to see the aggregate view of the processes, outputs, and strategies of your customers. The helicopter approach lets you move from strategic thinking (high level) down to tactical execution (low level). By moving from high to low levels, you can align your outputs accordingly at each level.

Sales Machine Approach

With this mental model, consider professional selling like a machine. The sales machine with many interrelated parts must work together for you to become a trusted advisor. The sales machine approach lets you look at your job in the best- and worst-case scenarios. With this approach, visualize the perfect sales machine working flawlessly. For example, think of a series of interconnected gears with each gear representing an important piece of the overall system. If this were the case, you would have a gear for marketing, a gear for selling, a gear for buying, a gear for management, a gear for service/delivery, and so on. Now visualize the best way to make all the gears work together.

And now visualize the worst-case scenario. Identify all the ways in which the machine can be "broken" or "misaligned" in order to

FIGURE 6.5

Sales Machine Approach Mental Model

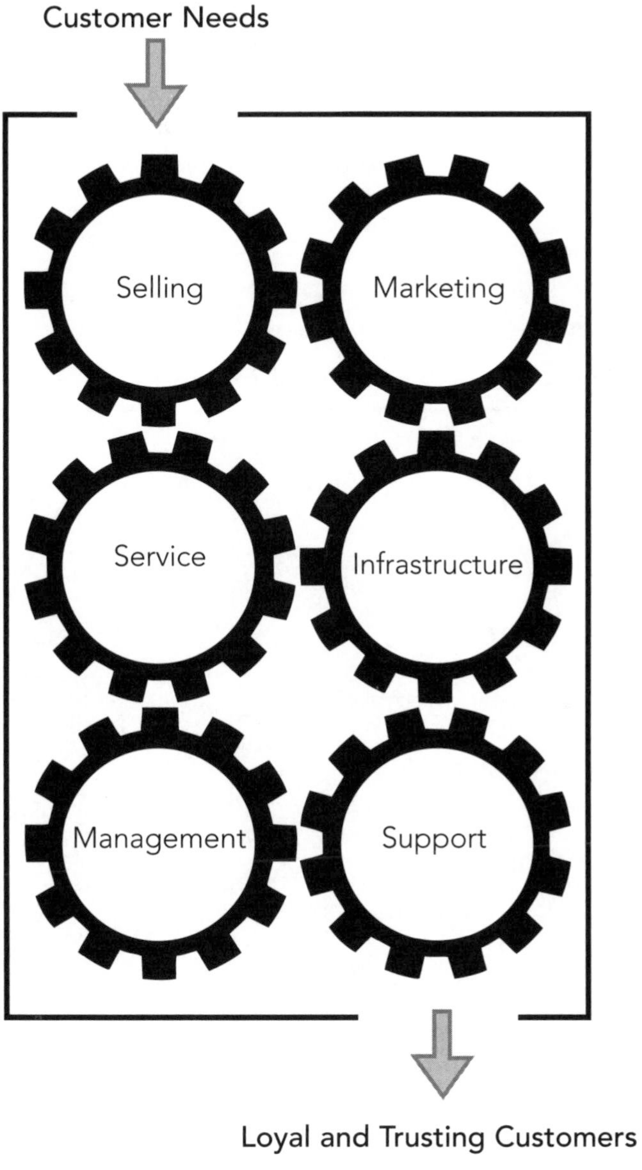

STEP 6

suggest appropriate fixes. Just like any other machine, you can identify preventative maintenance approaches as well as contingency plans if (and when) something should go terribly wrong.

Living Sales Organism Approach

In this model, view professional selling as a "living and breathing" natural system. Like most living organisms, you define the care, feeding, and raising of yourself and your surroundings. Recognize if the system is sick and identify the problems. Doing so will help you

FIGURE 6.6
Living Sales Organism Mental Model

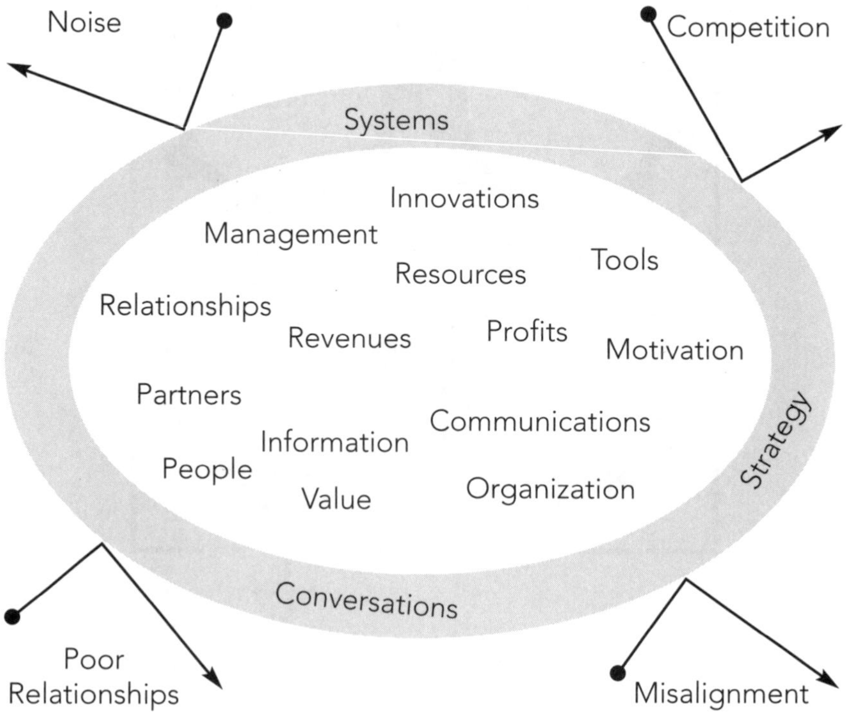

STEP 6

fix what is wrong and get the system back in working order. Much like a living cell, the sales system should be viewed as having a boundary with the goal to "let good stuff in" and "keep bad stuff out."

POINTER

The first rule is to break your own rules. If you don't like public speaking, speak in front of a large group. If you hate technical questions, become an expert. Going beyond your comfort zone is the key to becoming a well-rounded salesperson.
– Paul St. Louis, Field Sales Engineer, ifm efector, inc.

You can grow the selling system organically with the proper balance of nutrition and exercise. You can also protect the system from harm by providing the right level of protection to its most critical areas. With this approach, determine the best way to grow your sales system to accomplish what you want. This approach is also very reliant on the environment within which it operates.

With these mental models, it's important to recognize that they exist within the current way sales professionals operate. What if the selling world becomes even more dynamic? New mental models may have to adapt.

With the mental model(s) serving as a framework, find one (or more) that work for you. As you begin to create your own personal selling system, your mental models will help you. You will notice the following about this systems approach to defining your own personal selling system:

- Your mental model will help you understand the big picture.
- Your mental model can help you focus on what you can control while working within the larger system.
- You can identify yourself within the mental model. This will help you become more comfortable in what you're doing and what you're asked to do so that you become a better decision maker.
- You can explore every facet of your system, by writing it down, before you start trying to make changes to any one part.

The Sales Funnel Is Dead: A Systems Approach

By looking at professional selling with a systems approach, you will probably notice that the sales funnel approach to professional selling will fit within your personal sales system and mental model. The sales funnel approach is often used to help salespeople define prospecting, presenting, and closing activities related to the buyer. The sales funnel is a simple visual that contains the larger prospect universe at the top of the funnel, and the closed deals at the bottom of the funnel. The logic of the sales funnel is that the more prospects you put into the top of the funnel, the more deals you will close. Figure 6.7 depicts a typical sales funnel that many people believe is applicable to most industries.

FIGURE 6.7

Traditional Sales Funnel

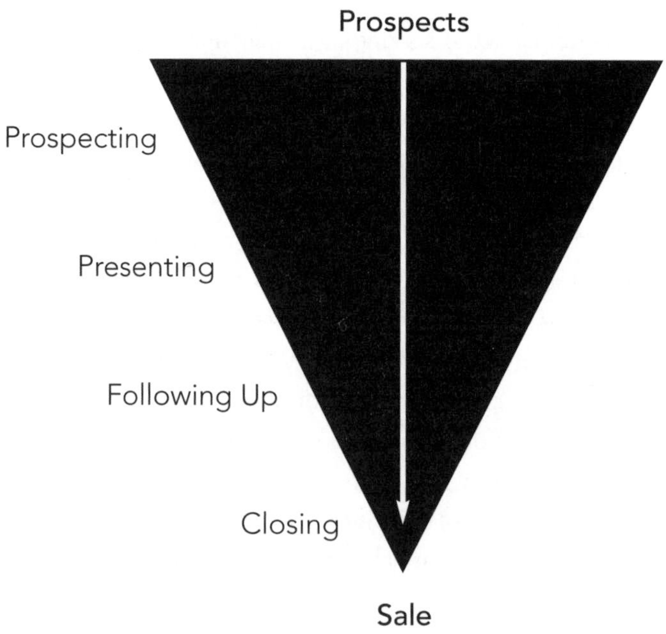

A word of caution about sales funnels: while the sales funnel can be a great place to start, it will not allow you to become a trusted advisor in and of itself. Think about it; when the deal is closed (from the seller's point of view), it's really just beginning from the buyer's point of view. Not only do most sales funnels look at selling only from the seller's point of view, but more important, they also don't take the larger system into account. This larger system contains marketing processes, delivery process, planning processes, measurement and evaluation processes, and communication processes. These processes cannot be oversimplified into a sales funnel, and they cannot be ignored if you are to become a trusted advisor to your customers. By using a systems view and customizing your personal selling system, you will have an important advantage that will set you apart from the competition. You cannot focus solely on the sales funnel.

Your Four-Stage Personal Selling Approach

Your personal selling approach should contain the primary stages of interaction that allow you to synchronize to the buyer's decision-making steps. It should contain all the processes necessary to achieve the sale (the sales process is one of many). Your personal selling approach should allow you to identify sales opportunities, plan account and process activities, manage your territory or portfolio, and integrate with your organization's marketing efforts.

To help simplify things, your personal selling approach should have three characteristics:

- **Repeatability**—Your personal selling approach should provide you enough of a framework to approach your professional interactions with buyers in a "scientific" manner. It should be easy to memorize and internalize, and should provide you with enough rigor to understand what changes are necessary in the processes you employ. Your approach should also help you understand how to learn from your mistakes. To do that, your personal selling approach must be fairly well defined, easy to use, and allow for the complexities of the selling system you identified earlier.

- **Scalability**—Your personal selling approach should allow you to appropriately focus your actions. To accomplish this, the approach should enable you to rapidly increase the span of control within your portfolio and accounts, while at the same time allowing you to treat each customer as a unique buyer who has their own buying experiences. You should be able to approach multiple prospects with multiple decision makers and synchronize to their buying processes. Likewise, you should be able to approach one decision maker and tailor your approach accordingly.
- **Flexibility**—Your personal selling approach should allow you to adapt to ever-changing market conditions as well as the decision-making processes of the buyer(s). To accomplish this, your process should help you be AGILE:
  - **A**daptable—Your approach should help you tailor your actions to meet buyer requests, keep up with changes in the buyer relationship, and respond to inputs.
  - **G**enuine—Your approach should help you be yourself. You shouldn't sell in a way that is not congruent with who you are and what you stand for. It should help you be authentic and real.
  - **I**lluminating—Your approach should help you find new ways of approaching challenges with your customers. It should help you be creative and enlightening to your customers (and to yourself) as you learn new approaches, ideas, and tactics.
  - **L**asting—Your approach should stand the test of time. It should help you build a long career as a trusted advisor.
  - **E**ffective—Your approach should be effective. It should work.

To help your personal selling approach be reliable, scalable, and flexible, there are four stages of the buying–selling experience that you need to manage:

- Stage 1: Initiating
- Stage 2: Communicating
- Stage 3: Implementing
- Stage 4: Assimilating

Each stage builds upon the next and allows you to best respond to the buyer's decision making and experiences. Each stage also enables you to tailor your personal selling approach in a manner that allows you to manage and measure results.

Stage 1: Initiating

The initiating stage focuses on gaining knowledge and defining customer demand.

- **Initiating processes** help you focus on gaining awareness and knowledge about the buying organization. To accomplish this, you will approach, identify, and target the buying organization through various tasks and activities.
- **Initiating activities** include creating messaging documents, profiling existing clients, and strategic marketing planning, such as conducting market research, prospecting, target account planning, account research, deal flow analysis, troubleshooting deals that have fallen through, and communicating to gain knowledge.
- Illustrative lists of initiating activities are shown in Table 6.1.

Stage 2: Communicating

This stage is where the bulk of buying and selling activity and dialogue take place. There is much more communication between you, your organization, and the potential buyers. This stage is extremely important, and it relies heavily on your ability to leverage the sale

TABLE 6.1

Initiating Stage of Your Personal Selling System

Phases and Processes	Typical Selling Activities (not all-inclusive)	Typical Buying (Client) Activities (not all-inclusive)
Approach Phase **Approaching Processes**	Planning, executing, closing, and reviewing Training and educational processes Competitive intelligence processes Reading and learning processes Communication processes	Strategic planning Trend analysis Organizational restructuring plan Gap analysis Corporate goals and strategy Merger/acquisition
Identify Phase **Identification Processes**	Planning, executing, closing, and reviewing Engage in active marketing toward generating sales	Needs assessment Comparison of needs against available resources Define budget and goals Gain needed approvals Establish an evaluation team
Target Phase **Targeting Processes**	Planning, executing, closing, and reviewing Collateral Industry reports or news Training delivered online National marketing efforts Capture planning Account planning Territory planning Organization actively seeks the business Free seminars for client/prospect internally	Vendor search Develop and issue requests for information Develop and issue request for proposal Gain needed approvals Determine key decision makers Establish buying committee

STEP 6

organization and sale competencies. The entire goal of this stage is to help the buyer understand the features, functions, benefits, and advantages of the solutions being discussed and then document this understanding in preparation for the next stage.

A key aspect of this stage includes eliciting information and needs from the prospective buyers through questioning and listening. More important, you will need to tailor a solution to meet their needs. This will require the ability to send and receive relevant messages. This stage is highly integrated to solve a problem.

- **Communicating processes** help you focus on documenting the buying organization's requirements, goals, and metrics. To accomplish this, you and your organization will support and accept the work of the buying organization through various tasks and activities. Some communicating processes include account planning, transaction management, project planning, presenting solutions, providing proof, documenting processes, consulting and fact finding, and role finding.
- Illustrative lists of communicating activities are shown in Table 6.2.

Stage 3: Implementing

This stage is where the product or service is actually fulfilled, created, or put into place. It is extremely important to understand that there is a handoff to the fulfillment function and/or the customer service function in this stage, depending on the selling model and products or service being sold. The focus of this stage is on execution. This means to properly execute the agreed-upon features, functions, benefits, and advantages as they were discussed and documented in the previous stage.

A fulfillment function may be the manufacturing plant, the software implementation team, or the installers in this stage. If the documentation isn't right and if you have not properly set the correct expectations in this stage (including documentation), then there is a chance the products or services will not be implemented and installed as planned. This will create unnecessary rework

TABLE 6.2

Communicating Stage of Your Personal Selling System

Phases and Processes	Typical Selling Activities (not all-inclusive)	Typical Buying (Client) Activities (not all-inclusive)
Support Phase **Supporting Processes**	Planning, executing, closing, and reviewing Testimonials Case studies Market trends in their industry Examples of other projects Example "project plan" templates Sharing of knowledge internally Show the accumulated wisdom Show the methodologies that will help them succeed Show the proof that can help them succeed Identify goals Discuss project scope, quality, risk management, communication, resources Discuss timelines Define expectations	Develop evaluation criteria Review responses Set up seller presentations Evaluate responses and presentations Determine return on investment criteria Determine key user criteria Align budgets
Accept Phase **Accepting Processes**	Planning, executing, closing, and reviewing Create memo of understanding Set performance measurements Discuss investment figures Matrix the data elements for selection and output Set the delivery methods Discuss operating procedures Documentation Creating statements of work Creating initial project documentation Developing training and implementation plans	Select seller Conduct negotiations Discuss implementation concerns Assign project manager and support team Begin internal alignment for implementation

and/or an unsatisfied customer. The key is the customer service and fulfillment functions must be in alignment with the salesforce to ensure they understand what took place.

- **Implementing processes** include education planning, risk management planning, communication planning, quality assurance plans, fulfillment processes, change management processes, service processes, feedback on new products and service features, and communication processes.
- Illustrative lists of implementing activities are shown in Table 6.3.

TABLE 6.3

Implementing Stage of Your Personal Selling System

Phases and Processes	Typical Selling Activities (not all-inclusive)	Typical Buying (Client) Activities (not all-inclusive)
Commit Phase Committing Processes	Planning, executing, closing, and reviewing Get the signature Introduce (in person or on phone) customer service and PM points of contact Set up review schedule Set up a kickoff meeting PM person discuss training schedule Go back and reconfirm what the customer really wants	Signs contract Discusses startup implementation Organizes for startup implementation Identify measures of success Set up reviews and measures
Fulfill Phase Fulfillment Processes	Planning, executing, closing, and reviewing PM responsibility Solution created and "happens" Delivering training Aligning the organization to achieve up-sell, cross-sell targets	Establish requirements Discuss impact Supply resources needed Develop change management plan Manage risk Implement

Stage 4: Assimilating

The focus of this stage is on measuring. This means to develop metrics, return on investment measures, customer feedback mechanisms, and so on that provide tangible proof of success. By proving this success, you and your organization can begin to build on short-term wins, develop long-term relationships, and expand by offering new products or services, or value-added solutions that enhance the customer's business.

- **Assimilating processes** that may be found in this stage are win–loss reviews, return-on-investment procedures, objective measurement processes, quarterly reviews with the customer, feedback processes for new product features, and in-depth account planning to capture new business within the existing account.
- Illustrative lists of assimilating activities are shown in Table 6.4.

Increase Your Sales Effectiveness

Now that you have a mental model, as well as the four stages of your personal selling system, how do you know if your approach is working?

STEP 6

TABLE 6.4

Assimilating Stage of Your Personal Selling System

Phases and Processes	Typical Selling Activities (not all-inclusive)	Typical Buying (Client) Activities (not all-inclusive)
Protect Phase Protecting Processes	Planning, executing, closing, and reviewing Customer surveys conducted Creating and delivering ROI proof Customer satisfaction surveys	Monitor performance Tracking Creating metrics of measurement Understanding of customer satisfaction and loyalty
Expand Phase Expanding Processes	Cross-sell activities and planning Support with superior customer service after the sale	Has a dedicated project or commodity team for your solution Look to selling organization for "first right of refusal" for additional work

To customize your personal sales system, assess yourself against five types of sales effectiveness in terms of critical work-related outputs and how well they support your sales goals. These five levels include

- effective sales strategies
- effective sales processes
- effective sales conversations
- effective sales technology
- effective sales performance.

Effective Sales Strategies

Effective sales strategies start with sales science—that is, *what* you are doing. Many sales professionals have spent countless hours defining approaches, methodologies, and processes for selling. They've worked hard at finding out what buyers want and tried to sell by making a sales presentation, utilizing negotiation techniques, or leaving a compelling voicemail.

However, the key to being effective is staying focused on the definition of value. By isolating the definition value (as your customer defines it) as a pivot point in time, you can build the "science" necessary to control as many variables as possible. Take notice of what went well and what didn't work as well as you had hoped during the sale. By taking time to reflect and understand why missteps failed, you can avoid future problems. No matter how simple the product or complex the solution, you will need to be effective at listening, questioning, and influencing.

Effective Sales Processes

Once you understand *what* you're trying to do, it's time to figure out *how* to do it. The most successful sales professionals work hard to understand what occurs between the buyer and seller within an individual transaction. By analyzing this information, they find what works and define a series of unique, repeatable steps that lead to closing more transactions. Focus on how sales work is accomplished to understand what it takes to sell effectively and close more transactions—then develop your own personal selling approach to cope with the higher level of complexity involved in sales these days.

Effective Sales Conversations

Once you have a sales process that works for you, it's time to focus on the conversations you are having. If you're approaching conversations from a transaction focus, move to a relationship focus. This change will have a dramatic effect on your progress to become a trusted advisor.

How is this accomplished? Assess your conversations and broaden your focus beyond limited issues. Begin facilitating a buying decision through a more consultative selling approach; for example, by helping buyers with solutions to solve business problems, you become more ingrained with the client's business and provide more protection for your relationship with the buyer. Another strategy to consider involves engaging multiple stakeholders so you are not subject to the whims of one decision maker.

Effective Sales Technology

Once you have solidly defined the science, standardized the process, and cultivated the right conversations for maximum influence, it's time to focus on technology. Some sales professionals struggle to cope with the Internet boom and scads of technology solutions to manage knowledge. Use technology to speed up your reaction time to market trends and to keep abreast of important industry news. Knowledge of this type of information enables you to be more strategic and develop a deeper understanding of your buyer(s).

Regardless of your current technology—from personal computers, handheld devices, customer relationship management system, or salesforce automation tool—the goal is to leverage technology to correctly assess the initial needs of the customer, deliver and fulfill a product or service, and process invoicing to create the best possible transaction experience for your customer.

Effective Sales Performance

With a solid foundation of science, process, conversations, and technology properly laid, the next step in your effectiveness journey focuses on improving performance. Despite the myriad forces of change driving business today, understanding and consulting with buyers in pursuit of mutually beneficial solutions is still a relevant approach.

The most successful sales professionals build and renew customer relationships, monitor and understand buyers' changing needs, and deliver ongoing value. This approach is difficult to implement consistently in a dynamic, constantly changing sales environment, but success comes with a holistic understanding of your own knowledge and skill.

Because buyers demand unique answers rather than a cookie-cutter approach to their unique problems, you need to customize and personalize your own selling approach. The five types of effectiveness can help you build customer satisfaction and loyalty. Now that you have a better understanding of the sales system and how to become effective, you need to put it all together.

In summary, this step described processes and strategies to create your own personal sales system, which is important to becoming a successful sales professional. Focus your attention on the buyer's particular situation, and enable yourself to ask the right questions, offer the right solution, and manage the complexity of the buyer–seller relationship. Keep in mind that you *must* create a repeatable, sustainable, and reliable personal sales system that works for you. By following this approach, you can create processes, tools, and strategies that all work together to help you become a trusted advisor.

The next step, Step 7, Accelerate Revenue, focuses on becoming a trusted advisor by leveraging creativity, employing exceptional listening skills, developing creative solutions, and building trust through ethical behavior.

WORKSHEET 6.1

Worksheet Documenting Your Personal Sales System

No matter which mental model you use, you will have to define the most important actions required to achieve success and document them for each stage. More important, you will have to identify and document the activities of your buyer for each stage. To do so, you will need to determine what specific questions to ask about their processes in order to

- learn how to synchronize to them
- help them advance to the next phase.

My Primary Mental Model:______________________________________

Phases and Processes	My Selling Processes	Typical Buying Processes
	Initiating Stage	
Approach Phase	Actions required	Activities witnessed
Approaching Processes	Resources needed	Questions to ask
Identify Phase	Actions required	Activities witnessed
Identification Processes	Resources needed	Questions to ask
Target Phase	Actions required	Activities witnessed
Targeting Processes	Resources needed	Questions to ask

STEP 6

Worksheet 6.1, continued

Phases and Processes	My Selling Processes	Typical Buying Processes
	Communicating Stage	
Support Phase	Actions required	Activities witnessed
Supporting Processes	Resources needed	Questions to ask
Accept Phase	Actions required	Activities witnessed
Accepting Processes	Resources needed	Questions to ask
	Implementing Stage	
Commit Phase	Actions required	Activities witnessed
Committing Processes	Resources needed	Questions to ask
Fulfill Phase	Actions required	Activities witnessed
Fulfillment Processes	Resources needed	Questions to ask

continued on next page

Worksheet 6.1, continued

Phases and Processes	My Selling Processes	Typical Buying Processes
Assimilating Stage		
Protect Phase	Actions required	Activities witnessed
Protecting Processes	Resources needed	Questions to ask
Expand Phase	Actions required	Activities witnessed
Expanding Processes	Resources needed	Questions to ask

SECTION THREE

OVERVIEW

How to Be a Trusted Advisor

Professionally managing the intersection between buyer and seller while delivering value at every point helps set you apart as a trusted advisor. Think about the role of an information technology (IT) sales representative. This type of sales professional has a territory that he or she calls on to discuss the features and benefits of solutions within the portfolio. In this situation, the IT sales rep has a precious two to three minutes to "gain interest" in any selling situation. Not only that, the IT field moves so rapidly that this sales professional must be constantly learning and developing technical expertise as well as selling expertise. Often asked to manage multiple relationships on both the buying and selling side of the transaction, this professional must prioritize activities, make the right decisions, and manage change at an unprecedented rate.

I define a trusted advisor as someone who can earn a buyer's trust, build relationships, and give effective advice about specific business challenges. Trusted advisor status is given to you by those around you. It's acquired by gaining confidence and credibility. It's not just about following a sales process; it's how you go about it. This level of professionalism comes from

- Step 7: Accelerate Revenue
- Step 8: Communicate Effectively
- Step 9: Manage Your Sales Organization
- Step 10: Develop World-Class Competencies

STEP SEVEN

Accelerate Revenue

OVERVIEW

- Cultivate creativity
- Develop listening skills
- Engage in ethical decision making
- Ethics case studies

Perhaps you know someone who you think is a great sales professional. What makes him or her a professional in your mind? Is it flexibility, an ability to create something new, or the way he or she is able to "fill in the blanks" in a certain situation? Because a sales professional is an effective and efficient trusted advisor, let's look at how they are able to continuously outperform and attain better results than most other people. The key is an ability to leverage creativity, listening skills, and great ethical decision making that work together to accelerate revenue.

Cultivate Creativity

For most people, the word *creativity* equates to a free-thinking, no-holds-barred expression of one's inner self (for example, painting, pottery, or poetry). Admittedly, using the word creativity anywhere near the sales process probably makes your manager a little nervous! Why? Because most sales managers have worked hard to instill some form of rigor into their sales organization. These same managers might not look forward to managing 10 to 15 free-thinking, no-holds-barred

POINTER

I believe that it is very important for new and seasoned salespeople to really listen to what the client is saying. There are too many times when salespeople try to sell the client something they think they need rather than what they really want. The client will tell you, just listen.
– Scott Bernard, VP of Sales, Medical Devices

salespeople who want to express their inner-self every chance they get.

Two points can be made about the above definition of creativity. First, the ability to create is not creativity—it's actually just potential that needs to be realized through action. Thinking creatively and creating new ideas doesn't mean much until something takes place or some action is taken. Second, the extent to which we can create is directly related to our past experiences (and oftentimes, our failures). The broader and deeper your knowledge, the more creative potential you will have. Creative potential is severely limited by lack of knowledge about one's profession.

To handle the chaotic world of professional selling, creativity is a great skill to have. Not only can it be a competitive advantage that helps you differentiate yourself, but it is also required to become an effective salesperson. To be effective in the sales process, you have to be creative. The best definition of creativity as it applies to the sales process is from a book called *The Medici Effect* by Frans Johansson, who defines creativity as "something that is new, valuable, and realized." So, ask yourself, does the buyer want you to bring something new, valuable, and real to the conversation? Absolutely! Buyers don't want promises; they want results. They don't want a payment; they want a return on investment. They don't want something they've already thought of; they want something new. Creativity defined in this manner can build trust and help you transition from salesperson to sales professional. Following are examples of what creativity might look like for you.

New—For an idea or solution to be creative, it also has to be new—and not just new to you. It's not you who defines whether or not something is new (and creative)—it's the buyer. If you approach the buyer in the same fashion as 20 other salespeople (all following the same sales process), then you're not doing anything new. If you're offering a solution that five other companies can provide, that's not new either. If your solution adds one or two features or benefits to an existing, well-known approach, that's not new (it might be innovative, but it's not new). Real creativity requires a risk and it often requires a new way of thinking. Albert Einstein once said "the problems that exist in the world today cannot be solved by the level of thinking that created them."

Valuable—For an idea or solution to be creative, it also has to be valuable. Since valuable is a subjective word (what I think is valuable, someone else might not think is valuable at all), the key is to look at the word *valuable* as a measure of relevancy. Something is valuable to me if it's relevant to me. Something is valuable to you if it's relevant to you. For something to be valuable to your client, it has to be relevant. For example, if I approached you in 1999 with a small product you could carry anywhere that allowed you to put a bunch of songs on it, listen to it, and easily navigate from one song to the next, you would have probably said, "So what?" or "What's in it for me?" In fact, you probably would have thought it wasn't creative at all (it's been done before). Fast forward to the launch of the Apple iPod™ and notice the worldwide movement it started. What was different about it? The difference was the way in which Apple™ was able to make the iPod relevant (and therefore valuable) in the eyes of the customer.

Realized—The reason why the Apple iPod was creative was because they made it happen. More important, the device spurned a whole new era of creativity around accessories, applications, and the way an entire industry interacts with the consumer. Digital downloads were unheard of five years before Apple's iTunes application became the number one seller of music downloads in the world. The bottom line is if the idea for the iPod existed solely in someone's head, and was never "sold" to anyone, it wouldn't have revolutionized the music or electronics industries. This type of phenomenon is not new. Salespeople have spurned many innovations in society. Think about how business has changed over the past 100 years—from the sewing machine and the cash register to the development of digital books and music—creativity was realized through understanding the buyer and helping them realize something new and relevant.

Develop Listening Skills

More and more, sales success requires you to talk less and listen more. When done correctly, listening effectively is one of your most powerful selling skills. When you speak, you give up power. When you listen on purpose, you are empowered to provide your buyer with specific benefits from you, your product or service, and your company. You need to learn how to benefit the most from every interaction you have with every person you meet—whether that person is a prospect, customer, friend, or even your boss.

> **POINTER**
>
> Are you really listening to the prospect, or just waiting for your chance to talk?
>
> *– Jake Atwood, President, Ovation Sales Group*

Keep in mind that communication is a two-way street. The responsibility rests with both parties. Listening, however, tends to get short-changed in terms of development because sales professionals assume they already know how to listen. After all, the mechanics of listening appear so simple. One individual speaks; another individual hears and responds. But there is a big difference between hearing and listening. Hearing refers to the physical perception of sound, while listening is a complex combination of hearing, seeing, comprehending, and interpreting communication.

In the world of selling, poor listening skills can be costly and affect performance by wasting selling time, processing inaccurate orders, losing sales, making incorrect assumptions, confusing the client or internal staff members, incorrectly setting customer expectations, and under-delivering. Alternatively, listening with full attention and commitment leads to greater sales, productivity, excellence, smoother relationships, collaboration, sharing, creativity, and innovation.

The good news is that effective listening is an acquired skill. Just as a salesperson can improve his or her verbal or presentation skills with conscious, deliberate practice, poor or mediocre listening skills can also be improved. However, improvement does take time and practice. Assessing your listening skills begins with self-examination. How do you relate to other people? Are you empathetic?

The key of becoming an effective listener is to develop an awareness and control of your own emotions. Nothing prohibits your ability to listen accurately and objectively more than strong emotion. If you are angry, you may misinterpret what the other person is telling you, casting the message in a negative light to match your mood. If you are sad or depressed, you may tune out the conversation. The first step to understanding your emotions is to pay more attention to them.

Once you begin paying attention to your feelings, examine a bit further. For example, keep a log of situations that provoke you. Describe the situations and the people involved as well as your feelings and responses. Look for patterns and embrace this insight to identify situations, events, and individuals that interfere with your ability to listen effectively.

One method to cultivate optimal listening is to apply Steil's sensing, interpreting, evaluating, and responding (SIER) model, which is described in greater detail in *Listening Leaders: The Ten Golden Rules to Listen, Lead and Succeed.*

In general, listening takes a lot of mental preparation. Consider the following tips when working on becoming a better listener.

- Recognize that powerful listening begins with deciding to really listen; listening is an inside-out job.
- Recognize that the more you understand your own thoughts, feelings, and actions, the more you will understand other people. Self-knowledge is the way to deeper empathy.
- After a challenging conversation that did not go as you had hoped, reflect on what happened and determine what you might do differently next time.

- Realize that you cannot fake listening and always strive to be genuine.
- Even when you do not like or agree with someone, view that person in the light of unconditional positive regard.
- Put yourself in the speaker's shoes to the best of your ability. Empathy fuels listening and is the ability to really see, hear, and understand others from their perspective.
- Recognize that if you are truly listening, your nonverbal communication will convey that. You will maintain good eye contact, an attentive body position, supportive hand gestures, and so forth.
- Recognize that every time you really listen, you strengthen your relationship with the speaker.
- Summarize the other person's views before sharing your own.
- In a conflict situation, use listening whenever the other party is emotional. When emotions run high, problem solving becomes difficult until the other party feels truly heard.

Engage in Ethical Decision Making

With impatient customers armed with knowledge about a seller and his or her competitors, sales professionals not only have to provide information, correctly assess client needs, handle objections, and send proposals, they also need to understand the kind of relationship the customer expects. Not only do these professionals need to adeptly handle all of the aspects of "selling," they also need to nurture the relationship or risk putting the business in danger.

> **POINTER**
>
> At first, don't get too bogged down in trying to understand the sales cycle, the buying cycle, and the other complexities of the sale—just ask more questions and listen carefully. Even seasoned salespeople need to learn to do this more. *– Emma Stevens, Sales Manager, Dialemma Solutions*

The profession of selling is uniquely positioned to provide services that directly deliver on the brand promise of the company. The brand promise is the perception of the selling organization in the eyes of the buyer. Because salespeople span boundaries between organizations, they have the potential to wield a lot of power. That power can be used in many different ways, including helping clients

- understand the competitive environment
- attain the products or services they need
- define their requirements.

As in any position of power, there are chances for abuse. In professional selling, the abuse of this power can occur because salespeople have the ability to help facilitate transactions between organizations. This is obviously a form of power (money).

POINTER

Listen with the intent to listen, not with the intent to speak. Ask a targeted, well-thought-out, open-ended question, then shut up and listen. Ask for permission to take notes. Taking notes forces you to focus on the speaker and the message. If you learn to listen, you will place yourself in an elite category of sales professional. This rare group can truly listen, understand, and apply what they have learned toward a mutually beneficial solution.
– Davey Moyers, Managing Partner, The Moyers Company

Unfortunately, this power often causes heartburn to some when thinking about salespeople. Other professions with power (such as judges, police officers, and even doctors) have a much higher standing regarding the ethical perceptions of the general population—the major difference is the lack of perceived "professionalism," especially in the lack of a widely recognized sanctioning organization and globally acceptable ethical code.

The Ethical Decision Making Triad

Given the perception that sales and marketing professionals are in some of the most unethical professions, how do you know when you're bordering on making an unethical decision?

Think of ethics as a three-pronged approach that you can test when working with prospects and clients. As illustrated in Figure 7.1, the ethical decision making triad provides a three-part test to determining if a given decision or action is ethical—that is, it will help you make the right decision, even when nobody is looking! The three-part test involves answering the following questions:

- **Is it legal?**

  The term *legal* should be interpreted broadly to include any civil or criminal laws, any state or federal regulations, any industry code of ethics, or any company policy. If salespeople don't know or have doubts about the legality of what they are doing, they should ask their management team and/or the legal department.

- **Is it moral?**

  Is it rational, as opposed to emotional, and balanced so that there are no big winners or big losers? Is it fair to

FIGURE 7.1

The Ethical Decision Making Triad

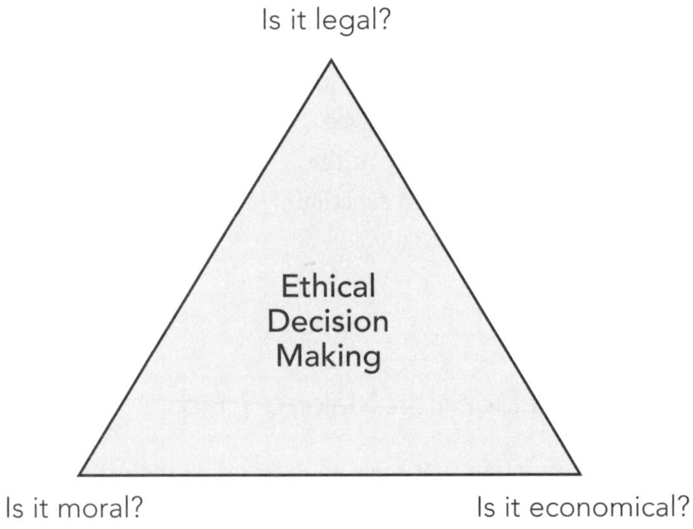

STEP 7

both the selling organization and the buying organization? Is it fair to the individual buyer, to the sales professional, to the advertiser, to the various communities, and to the companies involved? Is it fair to all the sales stakeholders?

- **Is it economical?**
  Is it economical for the organization? Is it a good business deal that makes sense from a business perspective? Does the decision help drive the intended business results?

Why the need to focus on ethics? Because solid and lasting relationships are built on a foundation of trust, and becoming a trusted advisor is the foundation of your reputation. Trust comes from a customer's experience with the sales professional over time. For example, if customers are not confident that a salesperson will follow through on deliverables in a timely manner, they will be less likely to believe what the salesperson says is "true." Oftentimes, the fate of winning a sale rests with the customer's decision to trust you. Therefore, any form of dishonesty (even those seemingly harmless white lies used to save face or avoid uncomfortable or embarrassing situations) needs to be avoided at all costs!

POINTER

Every time you communicate to a customer, the possibility of losing the deal exists . . . so make sure you spend most of your time listening.
– Dr. Wayne Neale, Founder and CEO, Professional Sales College

STEP 7

Ethics Triad Questions You Can Ask Yourself:

- Would my parents be proud of me if they knew what I was about to do?
- How would I react if I were spending this money?
- Would I stake my professional reputation on the decision I make?
- Is this legal, economic, and moral?
- Who, if anyone, will be hurt by my decision?
- Is it fair to everyone—to both sides, to the consumer, to the salesperson, to the various stakeholders, and to the company?
- What if everybody did this?

Ethics Case Study 1

Beth sells application development and design software for a large multinational company. For 12 months she has been working on an opportunity to fill an upcoming requirement for more than $50,000 in software for a local retailer. Her main contact with the retailer, Mr. Smith, is the leader of a purchasing team that will control the final decision. Mr. Smith is a professional buyer who has told her that he will follow the guidelines for purchasing (which include confidentiality of items such as vendor information, pricing, terms and conditions, and so on). He has been a "close to the vest" person during the whole process.

During a weekly sales meeting with her manager, Beth was asked about the software opportunity. Her manager wanted to know if it was progressing as planned or if she could foresee any delay in closing the deal. Beth replied by saying everything was going "as planned" and that the final proposal would be ready to submit to Mr. Smith by the due date. All she needed was one more meeting with Mr. Smith and his technology team leader to get more details about how the software would be installed and the staff would be trained.

Because it was Friday, Beth and her sales manager needed to go over next week's activities. When Beth looked in her palm pilot at the following Monday, she was shocked to find that the due date for the final proposal was the upcoming Monday (February 28), not the following Monday! It's now Friday afternoon, February 25, and she is panicked. She asks her manager if she can postpone this portion of the conversation to "attend to something" and excuses herself from her meeting.

She quickly phones Mr. Smith, who indeed confirms that the deadline is February 28. Her next question was to determine if an extension could be granted, but Mr. Smith says no because the other two vendors have already turned their bids in to him.

Beth thinks she can work on finishing the proposal over the weekend. She then asks if she can schedule an appointment with him and his technology leader for later today in order to get the remaining information she needs. Mr. Smith states that his day is filled with other important appointments and he doesn't have any additional time for a meeting.

With that, the phone conversation ends and Beth is left in her cube to determine her best course of action. About an hour later, Mr. Smith phones her with an idea. He really feels bad for her and suggests that maybe they could get together over the weekend, perhaps for dinner Saturday night. He goes on to say that he could even bring along the other proposals that contain the detailed technical information she is lacking in order to complete her bid and to "see what she's up against."

What is the best course of action for Beth to take?

1. Give up on the account because there is nothing she can do and she is going to lose the deal anyway.
2. Go to dinner with Mr. Smith to get the information she needs and see what the others are proposing.
3. Do the best she can on the proposal and submit it without the information she doesn't have, on time.
4. Set up a meeting after the deadline to gather the appropriate information. Submit the proposal even though it is late.

Tip! The "answers" to this case study are in Appendix E on page 251.

Ethics Case Study 2

John is a salesperson for a mid-sized information provider. He sells a database of business information and technology that other companies can use to market, track changes with other firms, and provide insight into vendors and suppliers.

John is briefed by internal sources about the trends, pricing, and products of competitors. This information is gathered from public sources (such as press releases, annual meetings, press coverage, and so on), but it is often not enough. John usually loses to the competition from DATA, Inc., the number one company in this industry. John has a powerful personal network that extends across the region. He has been selling for a long time and "knows everyone." Because he has access to important data, he is often asked to provide information on companies for his friends, which he gladly does for no charge. Lee is a new acquaintance of John's. They met through a "friend of a friend" who thought it would be good for the two to know each other. Lee and John agree to meet for dinner to get to learn more about each other's business needs and goals, and to determine if there is a way to help each other.

During dinner, a discussion starts regarding the information industry that John represents. John doesn't know that Lee is relatively new to selling and considers John a "guru." Lee wants to really impress John with his own network and seeks to gain John as a powerful extension of that network. After a lengthy discussion,

Lee realizes that a friend of his (Suzanne) is also in the same industry as John and works for one of his competitors—DATA, Inc.

Lee has been a friend of Suzanne's for many years and often met with her for advice. The two always shared information about each other's companies, with the agreement that they would not tell anyone else what was discussed. For the past year, though, Suzanne has become less and less accessible and stopped returning Lee's calls. Lee begins to think that John might become the next Suzanne and is eager to find a way to help.

As the conversation continues, John becomes more and more aware that Lee is very knowledgeable and he is impressed with Lee's ability to understand such a dynamic and broad industry. John shares the fact that he is having more and more trouble meeting quota. He's been particularly frustrated with DATA, Inc., and their ability to win almost every proposal against him. He asks Lee if he's heard of the new product called "Interactive Data Miner" being launched by DATA, Inc.

Lee knows a lot about the Interactive Data Miner product because Suzanne was involved in the focus groups and internal product development efforts with her company. She would often share the results of product reviews, focus groups, internal analyses, and competitive advantages of the product. In short, Lee knows nearly as much about this product as Suzanne does.

John has asked Lee for information that would be helpful and Lee has that information. What should Lee do?

1. Share the information about the product since it's gathered from a reliable source and would be helpful to John.
2. Say nothing to John about what he knows and shift the conversation.
3. Tell John that he does know a lot about the product, but cannot discuss it.
4. Since Suzanne isn't his friend anymore, tell John to ask questions and he will answer them with a "yes" or "no" only.

Tip! The "answers" to this case study are in Appendix E on page 251.

STEP 7

In summary, Step 7 focused on how becoming a trusted advisor means your clients have a great deal of trust in you as a sales professional. To gain that trust, your internal organization needs to support you in the sales process and support the implementation of the client's product, service, or solution. Sales professionals must often take leadership roles to drive internal organizational support as well as set and manage client expectations.

The next step to becoming a trusted advisor is learning how to communicate effectively by minimizing noise, developing effective questions, and optimizing your message.

POINTER

Listen—Too many salespeople worry about the numbers and what is in it for them. A good salesperson listens to his client. The salesperson must find out the needs of his client and deliver on them. If this is done well, the numbers will be there. Oftentimes, I see salespeople having a hard time cold calling. If the intention of the call is to ask questions about the needs of the client, as opposed to making a quick sale, then the call will be easier to make and the client will be much more receptive to the call and to the salesperson. All that is needed after the initial call is then to follow up based on the client needs that were discussed.
– J. W. Najarian, Commercial Real Estate Finance, Emerald Bay Investments, LLC

STEP 7

WORKSHEET 7.1

Worksheet Listening Assessment

Instructions: Want a better read on how well you listen? Rate yourself using this assessment to find out. To get a wider perspective, give copies of this assessment to coworkers, friends, family, and clients to learn their opinions of your listening practices.

To complete the assessment, rate the person being evaluated based on the following scale: 1 = Never, 2 = Rarely, 3 = Sometimes, 4 = Other, 5 = Always.

Person Being Evaluated: ____________________________________

Area	Rating
1. Gives the impression that he or she is fully listening.	1 2 3 4 5
2. Makes the speaker feel as if he or she is the center of the conversation.	1 2 3 4 5
3. Gives the speaker plenty of time to talk.	1 2 3 4 5
4. Refrains from interrupting the speaker.	1 2 3 4 5
5. Looks at the speaker with encouraging eye contact.	1 2 3 4 5
6. Does not fidget with objects or otherwise act distracted.	1 2 3 4 5
7. Helps keep the speaker on track with paraphrasing.	1 2 3 4 5
8. Probes for deeper understanding.	1 2 3 4 5
9. Does not finish the speaker's sentences.	1 2 3 4 5
10. Conveys an attitude of openness and sincerity.	1 2 3 4 5

Worksheet 7.1, continued

Area	Rating
11. Puts the speaker at ease, encouraging deeper sharing.	1 2 3 4 5
12. Asks questions that open up the discussion.	1 2 3 4 5
13. Asks questions to direct more discussion to a particular point, when helpful.	1 2 3 4 5
14. Asks questions to draw out emotion as much as fact.	1 2 3 4 5
15. Does not insert humorous remarks when the speaker is serious.	1 2 3 4 5
16. Refrains from "sneaking a peek" at his or her watch.	1 2 3 4 5
17. Smiles at the speaker and leans forward to convey interest.	1 2 3 4 5
18. Does not give the impression of "listening just for show."	1 2 3 4 5
19. Creates an atmosphere of trust and connection through listening.	1 2 3 4 5
20. Demonstrates empathy through listening.	1 2 3 4 5

NOTES

STEP 7

STEP EIGHT

Communicate Effectively

OVERVIEW

- Minimize the noise
- Hone your message
- Employ effective questioning techniques
- Master communication skills
- Present skillfully
- Propose solutions

Salespeople spend most of their time communicating, and often the content of the communication is highly repetitive. This repetition can lead to communicating without really thinking about the quality of the communication. In today's extremely competitive market, customers expect sales professionals to communicate at an exceptional level in all media—face-to-face, by telephone, and in written communication. They expect sales professionals to be extremely articulate about products, artful about inquiry, polished in their presentation skills, and both direct and authentic.

Understanding all facets of communication can propel average salespeople to the top of the sales rankings—and this step focuses on the key concepts and tips to help get you there. The most successful sales professionals actively work on their communication skills and reflect on what can be improved after every client meeting. To make these strategies work for you, minimize noise, hone your message, employ effective questioning techniques, and master how to interpret what your clients aren't vocalizing but what they are really saying through nonverbal communication.

Minimize the Noise

Generally speaking, anything that interferes with communication can be called "noise." Noise can be a distraction, a misinterpretation, different meanings assigned to the same words by different people, or quite literally noise from an open window or an office next door that disrupts communication.

Noise represents a breakdown in the communication process and can occur at any time. You can minimize noise by following these principles:

- Always remember what's important. It's not the message you send or what you communicate, per se. It's really about how that message or communication was *received* by the recipient. Perception is reality. If they didn't "get it," then it's your fault, not theirs.
- Never assume that your message is perceived in an unbiased manner. All information is perceived according to the receiver's needs, personality, emotions, and point of view.
- Do assume that all information has implications regardless of how objective you feel the message is. Your goal should be to give the information in the format necessary for the buyer to make a decision.
- Noise occurs most often because the sender and receiver of the communication don't share enough in common (professionally or personally).

Hone Your Message

Remember that buyers know why you're talking to them. It's not a secret that your job is to attempt to understand a need and fill it. They know you're a "salesperson," no matter what your job title is (or else they probably wouldn't be talking with you in the first place). The goal should be to keep your communication relevant and professional. You can use communication to achieve the following objectives:

- set expectations
- create awareness

- develop someone's knowledge of the solution
- gain commitment.

This is easier said than done. To accomplish these objectives, you'll need effective questioning techniques, listening skills, and presentation skills.

Employ Effective Questioning Techniques

Buyers will attempt to gather facts that support their initial conclusions about a solution and disregard other facts that support different conclusions. Therefore, past experiences and thoughts are important to understand by using probing and open-ended questions.

While most of your competition continues to talk their way out of sales, you will learn to ask your way into accelerated sales success. Learn to leverage the power of question-based selling. You will find out more about your prospect and their wants or needs while building credibility, establishing yourself, and positioning your company and solution as the only remedy to their specific situation.

There are many directions your questions can go in a meeting. To stay grounded, be sure to

- determine the right people who can provide you the correct answers you need
- identify what you absolutely need to know about your target before you make your first contact
- develop the right questions that allow you to illicit the information you need while building credibility and providing you the strongest competitive advantage.

The best questioning technique I have found is the "SPIN" selling methodology created by Neil Rackham and Huthwaite International. In the book *SPIN Selling*, SPIN is an acronym for **S**ituation, **P**roblem, **I**mplication, and **N**eed-payoff questions. The methodology was derived from the multi-year effort Rackham undertook in which he analyzed more than 40,000 sales interviews in 27 countries and studied 116 factors that might play some part in improving sales performance.

His conclusion was that exceptional sales performers use four types of questions, which are categorized by the function they provide in the sales process, to uncover specific information, problems, needs, or implications.

- **Situation questions** are used to gather background information and understand the complete context of the transaction experience.
- **Problem questions** are used to explore the customer's concerns and problems and more fully understand them.
- **Implication questions** are used to develop and link apparently isolated problems by examining their cumulative effect on specific areas of the prospect's business.
- **Need-payoff questions** are used to encourage the customer to expressing their concerns and consider the benefits of solving his or her problems.

Through your questioning process, the buyer may decide to stop looking elsewhere because he or she trusts you and is willing to accept the fact that your company can provide an alternative that looks like it might work for them. Another part of questioning will be to determine what the buyer has been hearing about your solution and from what sources. They will often believe information they received from the greatest number of different sources.

In many organizations, there is a team of buying stakeholders who will look at the process of purchasing from you as a step-by-step incremental process. The decision (in and of itself) is just a "small step" in a larger process that could take many weeks or months. This is why you will know (in the next phase—accept) if someone is going to buy from you, even before they write the check.

POINTER

Asking great questions is the most important thing in sales. It's also the most fun! Once you've learned about your customers' needs, you must ask yourself which of your products or services can you offer that will create value, build a lasting relationship, and solve your customers' problems. If your solutions can't solve your customers' problems, walk away.
– Lee Porter, Sales Maven, Trebuchet Group

Only the buyer is able to work through the decision within his or her unique organization. However, you can help the buyer do this because you have a "macro" view and you are exposed to many more organizations where you can draw a broader set of best practices. In short, if you work at it, you could be a specialist in a given vertical market or product. With this knowledge you can help the client through their buying processes by ensuring you interview, present, or gather input from all key decision makers and stakeholders. You will need to discuss important milestones and a master timeline for delivery or implementation, and what the implementation strategy will entail.

Master Effective Communication Skills

When communicating—whether verbal or written—keep in mind that there are two dynamics at play—your communication style as a sales professional and the client's style. For example, some customers may be very interested in immediately drilling into the details, whereas others may need the bigger picture before they can engage in an in-depth discussion. In this situation, a detail-oriented sales professional will need to adjust his or her communication style to match that of the customer. This is a key tenet to embrace whether you are crafting written communications or engaging in face-to-face discussions.

Written Communication

Think about the scores of emails that both you and your clients must wade through every day. Who has time to read through rambling emails to try to figure out the point, what is being offered, or to answer questions?

More than ever, clients expect immediacy with regard to communication—including quick turnaround time for requests for proposals, as well as answers to questions or issues that crop up. Written communication, especially email, is the most challenging form of communication because it only uses about 7 percent of a salesperson's ability to communicate.

Sometimes it is easier to write a long email than a short one. Shorter emails can be difficult because there are several key points to cover. This leads to a dilemma. If the communication is too long, the customer may not read it all; if it is too short, the customer might misinterpret or not fully understand what you are trying to communicate.

When crafting any communication, the same basic formula applies.

- **Prepare**—Preparation is especially important for email. Easy to use and easily abused, email provides conveniences and challenges. The convenience: reaching the client directly and instantly. The challenge: misinterpreting important information.
- **Draft the message**—When creating a draft of the communication, be sure to personalize the opening and closing. Start with the big picture before moving to the detail; present your purpose, value, or request; and then recap the key points and identify next steps.
- **Check for unintended consequences**—Read the written draft and verify if the details you need to communicate are clear yet brief. At times, the brevity of written communications may not emphasize enough detail or the serious nature of a situation. Strike a fine balance between brevity and thoroughness.
- **Refine**—Refining a communication should focus on "does the message reflect your organization's personality, tone, and manner?"

Keep in mind that written communication is unforgiving because you don't have the advantage of tone of voice, body language, or surroundings. Once you have documented something in writing, it is permanent. In this type of communication, people are also usually less forgiving than in an oral conversation where people are often "thinking aloud." Email in particular is unforgiving because we do it quickly, thus creating opportunities for error in explicit language or implicit tone.

Although email can be interactive and affords some opportunity to ask for clarification, if a salesperson unintentionally offends the recipient, he or she may never get an opening to restate the message.

Voicemail

Everyone has left a voicemail at one time or another that they wish could be retracted or rerecorded. When communicating over the phone, several key points can help you craft effective voicemail messages. While voice tone is the critical component to effective communication, if you get flustered or nervous when leaving messages, consider the following:

- Think about your message before calling.
- If you ramble or get rattled, create a quick bullet list of the key points you want to communicate. Voicemail messages should indicate (1) who you are, (2) the subject or purpose of your call, and (3) what you are asking the client or prospect to do.
- Find a quiet location to leave the message. Nothing is more annoying than when someone leaves a voicemail message that is drowned out by background noise.
- Leave your phone number at the start of the message and again at the end of the message.
- Speak slowly when communicating your phone number. Write it down as you go so you can pause between numbers. Make sure you don't trail your voice off at the end of the number.
- Indicate the best time to reach you.

> **POINTER**
> People do business with people they like. Get them talking about themselves, listen for what their pain is, formulate in your mind how you could ease the pain, present your solution, and you will make the sale. Genuinely listen, care, solve, and follow up—and you will keep the repeat business.
> *– Jon Rhiddlehoover, Outside Sales Manager, U.S. Concrete, Inc.*

Verbal and Nonverbal Communication

Verbal communication can immediately engage or turn off your audience. Think about the satirical characters of "fast talking" sales professionals that you see on television. They talk so quickly to get in all of the features and benefits of their products that there is little two-way communication happening. It seems to be a nearly endless string of ramblings—and any value in the message is lost in the way it is presented. To perfect your verbal communication, consider the four Ps—pace, pitch, projection, and pronunciation.

- **Pace**—Skilled communicators adjust their rate of speaking to accentuate key points and engage the listeners. Although the average rate of speech is about 140 words per minute, to show enthusiasm or energy, try increasing the number of words per minute. When you need to make an important point perfectly clear or set expectations, try slowing down the rate to 100 words per minute. One trick: if you think your pace to too rapid, consider taping your conversations or "pitch," from the initiation of the conversation through to the close. To assess if your pace is appropriate, take one-minute intervals at different points during your conversation and count the number of words per minute.
- **Pitch**—There is nothing worse than a monotone conversation or discussion. When talking or presenting, avoid droning on and be sure to modulate the pitch of your voice up or down to accentuate more serious information, show your excitement, and appropriately set expectations.
- **Pronunciation**—If your clients have a hard time understanding what you're saying, it's as if you didn't say it at all. Exceptional diction, that is, speaking precisely, helps demonstrate that you are a polished professional and possess the gift of speaking clearly whether asking or answering questions and suggesting solutions.
- **Projection**—When talking with a group of clients or delivering a presentation, if they have to strain to hear what you're saying, you will probably lose their interest. Especially when presenting to a group, be prepared to ratchet up your voice

to ensure that folks in the back of the room can easily hear you and be sure not to inadvertently drop the volume after the first few sentences of your presentation.

Body language—meaning how you look and move—can enhance or undermine your clients' perception of you. Based on different studies, what you say accounts for only 10 percent of the effectiveness of your communication. Ninety percent is attributed to nonverbal communication, including gestures, eye contact (or lack thereof), and facial expressions.

Many new sales professionals struggle with effectively using their body language and gestures to enhance and not distract from their message. As a result, it is important to plan the key aspects of what you want to communicate in advance and think through the body movements to best emphasize your key points. When conducting a presentation, movement can be used to make a point or draw attention to key information. By moving in a purposeful way, you help to maintain the client's or group's interest and attention while keeping the presentation moving.

Be sure to use positive facial expressions when building trust and credibility with a client. For example, smiling, expressive eyes, a look of concern, empathy, and encouragement all help to convey that you are approachable, interested, and engaged in helping uncover the client's needs to provide value and a remedy for their pain.

Present Skillfully

Sales presentations are scripted (written) explanations of the value you provide to the prospect. They are usually a blend of visual (such as PowerPoint) and oral communications where the buyer expects you to share information that focuses on the benefits of what you are selling as it relates to solving their specific problems.

Presentations should be engaging and to the point. They should also begin with the most important benefits and continue in descending order of importance. It should only include pertinent benefits in regard to the current transaction experience, and should include appropriate, customized, and easy-to-understand illustrations, where applicable.

As part of the presentation, you may choose to prepare materials for your expected audiences and forums (such as handouts for larger audiences that might not be able to see your screen). Presentation highlights could include company history, best customers, benefits offered, and problems solved (solutions) and a list of potential questions to determine how serious the prospect is about buying (such as "What would happen if this problem wasn't fixed?").

Salespeople should set aside time to practice their presentations (using supplemental handouts or PowerPoint slides). This can be done alone or in front of a team, mentor, manager, or coach. Your presentation should also include a powerful conclusion that clearly illustrates the benefits your prospect will receive as a result of buying your solution now. To do this, you must believe in your product or service. You must also create a connection between your product or service and the prospect. Make the presentation relevant to your prospect. One of the most common mistakes people make when discussing their product or service is to use a generic presentation.

When analyzing the selling situation, you must determine why your presentation is essential in the first place. Knowing the situation will help you decide how to shape your content and choose

POINTER

After getting a lead (what sometimes may be the hardest part), you always have to start the communication with so-called open questions. This is best by phone or personal talk. Open questions are questions that cannot be answered by "yes" or "no"; for example, "What is the target of your new project?" At the end you have to summarize with closed questions such as, "You want to produce 10 boxes per minute, right?" Your questions should be like a funnel, narrowing to one simple aim: the quote or on-site demo of the stuff you want to sell.
– Thorsten Beierle, Graduated Engineer and Sales Manager, Data Translation

your style. In this analysis, you need to ask yourself the following questions:

- What is the need for the presentation?
- What will happen to the organization after the presentation?
- How does the presentation fit into the organization's situation?
- In what surroundings will you make your presentation?
- How does your presentation relate to your audience's actions?
- How can you help the organization?

An example of analyzing the situation would be to conduct background research on the presentation audience to find out what they do, how you can benefit them, and why they asked for your presentation. Analyzing the selling situation can also facilitate answers to other steps in the communication process.

Following are basic guidelines for presentations:

- Stand erect, and speak clearly and loudly enough to be heard in all areas of the room.
- Introduce yourself and the members of your sales team at the start of the presentation.
- Shift positions during your presentation, but don't rock or pace.
- Use visual words and physical descriptions as well as your visuals during the presentation.
- Speak directly to your audience, shifting your eyes every five or ten seconds. Continually make eye contact.
- Use your hands and arms only slightly, and then only for emphasis. Concentrate most of your energy into your facial and vocal expressions.
- Focus on your audience's body language and make certain you keep them interested. If people seem restless or it is apparent that you are losing their attention, change your pace or skip to a more interesting portion of the presentation.
- Don't worry about mistakes. They will happen no matter how many times you have made the presentation. Just don't amplify the mistakes to your audience—often they will go unnoticed.

Propose Solutions

In more and more complex or consultative selling situations, the buyer or the buying organization requires a proposal in order to clearly define and represent the commitment that both the buyer and the seller are making. As a result, the proposal is often a necessary requirement of reaching sales goals. Following are key points to keep in mind:

- A good sales proposal can help you advance the sales process. It can represent your best sales effort wrapped into a well-packed and branded representation of you and your company.
- If you're going to bother writing a proposal, make sure it is good or don't bother. It should be as good as (or better) than your best sales call with the customer.
- A proposal is actually a sales presentation in written form. It can commit you in writing and can sometimes be difficult to correct or clarify once it is out of your hands and in the hands of the buyer(s).
- Regardless of how good your proposal is, it doesn't replace the salesperson. It should be designed to complement your activities.
- Ideally, the proposal should be co-created with the buyer(s), and it should cover all the necessary points to help the buyer(s) move the process forward in their organization.
- A proposal can sometimes become passive. It may need your support so that action can be taken.

STEP 8

◆ ◆ ◆

To summarize, the most successful sales professionals have mastered communication skills on many levels—by minimizing noise, leveraging effective questioning techniques, and modeling exceptional verbal and nonverbal communication—to become a trusted advisor. The next step focuses on managing your sales organization and explores the many roles you are expected to play, how to set expectations, and how to run productive meetings to achieve defined objectives.

WORKSHEET 8.1

Present Effectively

Instructions: Fill in the blanks. This job aid will help you prepare for an upcoming sales presentation.

Knowing the Five Ws

Whom are you presenting to?

___

What are you presenting?

___

Why are you presenting (what does the audience want)?

___

When are you presenting?

___

Where are you presenting (what are the facilities and equipment like)?

___

Making Your Points

What are the main points of your presentation? What do you want the audience to walk away with? List at least three, but no more than five. These points make up the body of your presentation.

1. ___
2. ___
3. ___
4. ___
5. ___

continued on next page

STEP 8

Worksheet 8.1, continued

Fielding Questions

Most of the time, you can anticipate the questions an audience will ask you. Take the time to brainstorm the top five questions you think you will be asked and formulate your answers.

1. ______________________________

____

2. ______________________________

____

3. ______________________________

____

4. ______________________________

____

5. ______________________________

STEP NINE

Manage Your Sales Organization

OVERVIEW

- It's not the job title but the hats you must wear
- Manage expectations
- Run effective internal meetings
- Know the sales culture

Professional sales success as a trusted advisor often requires organizational support. That doesn't mean a token nod to the sales team by a department or a function; rather, it is an understanding of the processes that intertwine and work together to align to the market and to the buyers. While these processes can be organized in numerous ways, each process requires you, and oftentimes other colleagues, to be highly focused on the customer's definition of value.

The needs of your clients and the business you operate within will require you to be highly adaptable and flexible. What can you do to be adaptable and flexible throughout your organization while working together across departmental boundaries? More important, how can you assume a leadership position (no matter what your title is) and help others select, order, and align their actions in order to drive performance?

The challenge comes from the sales capacity created by your organization. Sales capacity is the organization's ability to create an ideal selling environment aligned to the customer where you, as a trusted advisor, can thrive. Because the selling environment surrounds you, it can help you succeed or it can impede your progress.

Have you ever heard the phrase, "Take a good person and put them into a bad system, and the system will win every time?" This holds true for sales professionals. No matter how good your personal selling system is, your hard work can be cancelled out by your organization's sales capacity. Conversely, your organization can be an accelerator of your success if you're lucky.

Unfortunately, the reality is that very few organizations have an optimum environment for you, as a trusted advisor, to operate within. In my opinion, many organizations create very little sales capacity for their sales professionals. The bottom line is sometimes you have to help your organization align to what you're trying to accomplish. This alignment needs to play out in multiple areas—from the marketing department to the service department and from management to the delivery and fulfillment function. It's time to think of your job in a slightly different way. This new way will help you focus on the positive, get things done, and make an impact no matter what kind of selling culture you must operate within.

It's Not the Job Title But the Hats You Must Wear

While you may have anguished over the job title you were given, forget it. Sales professionals know that it's not the title they get; it's the value they bring to their clients that really matters. Besides, sales job titles and sales roles are not the same thing.

Fundamentally, a job title represents a place on the organizational chart—a function that an employee carries out on behalf of the organization. By contrast, roles are the behavioral responses to the critical buyer–seller relationship and can literally change by the minute. Sales professionals can play many roles as they work hard to be trusted advisors.

Think of roles as the "hats" you must wear in order to engage in the sales process throughout a day, a month, or a year. Thinking of these different hats will help you manage the complexity and respond to the fluid and constantly changing demands around you.

Choosing the right role at the right time is the crux of the matter—correctly interpreting those internal and external demands and how to respond. Roles can help you attain trusted advisor status by identifying the best way in which to work more effectively with your customers (externally), as well as with individuals directly and indirectly responsible for driving revenue (internally). At the same time, roles can help you determine the best way to synchronize to the buying process. This is how high-performing sales professionals operate—but they can only do so if they are already equipped with the requisite knowledge, skills, and abilities to meet the demands of the roles that they must play.

The six key roles of successful sales professionals are consultant, strategist, developer, manager, analyst, and administrator.

Consultant

In this role you will

- leverage expertise and resources to build strong advisory relationships
- suggest best courses of action based on data and help with rational decision making
- guide the decision making of others, including internal or external customers
- recognize opportunities for products, services, or solutions to bring parties together to create a mutually beneficial relationship
- act as the point person in negotiating transactions, fulfilling documented agreements, and building the relationships that are essential to long-term partnering.

Strategist

In this role you will

- envision ways of operating or achieving goals that do not currently exist
- articulate the vision in a way that facilitates its transformation to an operational reality in response to challenges or opportunities
- apply or lead the application of innovative ideas and systems to create a competitive advantage for the organization.

Developer

In this role you will

- create business, organizational, or operational solutions or performance improvement initiatives by designing, developing, and delivering specific processes, systems, tools, events, or products intended to add value
- create or contribute to plans, specifications, or designs that guide individual, product, or process development activities.

Manager

In this role you will

- exercise direction and supervision of an organization or department
- control and allocate resources and budgetary expenditures, and enforces accountability and compliance of work-related policies and procedures.

Analyst

In this role you will

- collect, synthesize, deconstruct, and reconfigure information (such as ideas, facts, and raw data) to provide insight to others

- work with customers to determine and document business needs
- document requirements, processes, or methods in the most appropriate manner
- understand technology, systems, and tools for use within the sales environment.

Administrator

In this role you will

- perform procedure-based activities that are often scheduled on a regular basis or require documentation
- be involved with activities that require compliance to established processes, practices, or operational rules.

Wearing the Hats

Because the buyer–seller relationship can be chaotic, the solution that addresses a customer's need in one moment may not be applicable in the next. How can you make sure you respond in the best way? This is where the sales roles can really come to life. Consider the following examples:

Example 1—The phone rings and your sales manager is on the other end of the line. He asks, "What are you going to do about your new sales being down?" What should you do to get sales up? You have options that draw on different roles, depending on the reason for the downturn:

- Are sales down because you don't get enough one-on-one time with key decision makers? You might want to create more activity as a consultant.
- Are sales down because you have a lack of organizational support? You might want to create that capability as a developer.
- Are sales down because you are not managing your time well? You might want to drive some activity discipline as a manager.

- Are sales down because the market is declining? You may want to recalibrate your sales strategy with your manager to target different opportunities as a strategist.

Example 2—A customer sends you an email indicating that he or she is not happy. What should you do? Adopt the appropriate response based on the requirements of the buyer–seller relationship.

- Is the customer unhappy because an undiscovered need is not being met? You might want to spend some time guiding the customer through need recognition and offering possible solutions as a consultant.
- Is the customer unhappy because the buying organization has received an incorrect invoice and does not know how to fix it? You might walk the customer through the process to correct the error as an administrator.

Example 3—During a staff meeting, you are informed that "you must attend sales training" to increase sales revenue. What should you do? The answer depends on what your personal system requires in that situation:

- Are you able to document whether or not sales training will help you? Do you have visible metrics from the last sales training you attended that show return on the investment? Do you need to define other indicators of success (behavior change, increased knowledge, shorter sales cycles)? Then you need to be an analyst.
- Is the sales training going to "stick" after return to the job? Do you want to recommend that training be followed by on-the-job reinforcement? Then you might want to help the management team see the need for such a solution as a consultant.
- Does the training they want to send you to appear to fill a need you have? Then you might want to evaluate other solutions required as a developer.

Choosing the right role at the right time is truly the crux of the matter. You must learn to correctly interpret customer demands and respond accordingly. This is how you should strive to operate—

but you can only do so if you have already been equipped with the requisite knowledge, skills, and abilities to meet the demands of the roles that you must play as a trusted advisor (see Step 10).

Manage Expectations

A sales manager once advised me to "focus only on what you can control" within the sales organization. While I'm a proponent of doing the best job possible within the limits set by the organization, I believe that to become a trusted advisor means taking a leadership position with internal colleagues, no matter which department they are in.

Leadership is about influence—and the best way to influence your organization and your clients is through properly setting expectations. Let's face it—most people inside an organization don't understand what you do or how you do it—they just want results. If you find people within your organization who truly understand the roles you need to play and the competencies you need to have, make sure you latch on to them!

Regardless of the situation or job title, you need to be prepared to set and manage expectations—it's a requirement of being a trusted advisor. Proactively looking at the hats you need to wear helps you to properly manage expectations and position yourself for world-class sales excellence.

Managing expectations properly (via roles) also ensures that there are no surprises with key stakeholders. Different stakeholders have varying needs, demands, and requirements that keep you on your toes. Do you understand the politics of the situation? Who is leading the particular effort and what level of buy-in do they have at this point? What are you doing on the technical side? Change is hard enough and not setting expectations often wastes a lot of time.

Setting expectations internally also involves informing management of when you expect deals to close to accurately forecast what's in the pipeline, and to monitor and track revenue generation. In addition, it is just as important, if not more so, to set client expectations. Setting client expectations also involves every role discussed in this section in order to meet expectations while carefully defining business benefits that can deliver long-term business success internally and externally.

Selling Is a Team Activity: Working with Internal Groups to Execute Flawlessly

Becoming a successful sales professional involves being more than a team of one. It requires you to work effectively with various internal groups in order to effectively set customer expectations and deliver flawlessly. Some of the individuals and departments you may need to work with to properly set expectations include

- **Marketing**—The profession of selling is as much of a "subset" of marketing as it is a separate profession. Both occupations are separate but equal in driving revenue for an organization. When they work together successfully, an organization will achieve greater profits and drive more revenue. You can help marketing professionals tailor their marketing materials and design strategies to leverage sales competencies.
- **Management**—Many organizations, whether they sell services or solutions, rely on managers to define requirements, hire the right people, manage communication, and create the service offering for customers. You can help managers understand how to work with sales professionals to create the right service or product, define scope, manage risk, maintain quality, and manage processes that support sales success.
- **Human resources**—Human resources functions are critical to the success of a sales organization. HR compensation, hiring, and development practices for sales professionals must encompass the entire continuum of the sales transaction. The right talent must be hired into the best sales positions that fit individual strengths and weaknesses, and then those people must be developed and retained. You can help HR professionals provide proper assessment, compensation, and training practices for sales teams that support the revenue generation efforts of the company.

- **Customer service**—Customer service staff work alongside sales professionals to create a positive buying atmosphere and experience for customers. Customer service is a value-added service that is often integral to the success of the sale. You can help customer service professionals gain a deeper understanding of how sales team members articulate value.
- **Information technology**—Information technology (IT) and its deployment and support can make or break the effectiveness of a salesperson. IT professionals can enable the sales process and will often help troubleshoot sales calls from the field. You can help the IT staff provide you and your sales colleagues with technology that helps maximizes knowledge, skills, and abilities while navigating the steps of the sales process.
- **Production**—A production organization is the crucial business unit that produces what the sales professional is selling. This could be the actual manufacturing facility (for products), or the service organization that codes software, programs the database, or customizes the solution. You can help production teams understand the constraints often placed on sales team members and the context of the buyer–seller relationship.
- **Accounting/finance**—Accounting and finance organizations play a vital role in helping sales professionals price products and build a return-on-investment strategy that resonates with buyers. You can help accounting and finance professionals better understand how to streamline billing, collection, and finance functions for sales transactions.
- **Legal**—Legal support and administration of internal forms, documentation, and other paperwork is crucial to properly selling the product or service. Often an organization will provide some sort of legal support for the sales professional, or this function might be outsourced. Obviously, the more legal requirements placed on salespeople, the less time they have available for selling. You can help your legal team better understand how to proactively identify ways to help salespeople lighten their administrative workload to allow for more value-added and customer-facing activities.

Run Effective Internal Meetings

Research conducted by HR Chally, a sales consulting and assessment company, found the one thing buyers want from their salespeople more consistently then anything else is the ability to manage the selling organization's delivery of what was promised. One of the most effective ways to achieve this external expectation (what was promised) is to diligently set expectations and leverage your personal sales system to run an effective meeting with internal colleagues. Why? Because working internally to align to the buyer requires a "two hands on the wheel" approach. People's time is a valuable resource, both in terms of what it costs and in terms of what else they can achieve in that time. Your interaction with the people you meet with can help you achieve alignment to the customer's expectations. An effective meeting can bring focus to the critical aspects necessary to create internal alignment and achieve your goals. Identify one or two key outcomes that are critical for deeming a meeting a "success." This ensures that the meeting discussions and participants are focused on achieving specific goals in the shortest period of time.

> **POINTER**
>
> When I first started, my manager told me to always cover shipping for my customers, so that they would be more inclined to buy from me. Worst advice ever because it trained my customers to expect it. It took me over two years to get my customers out of that expectation. It makes me sick to think of all the profit I lost for paying for all that freight. If you are good at selling yourself, a customer won't care about having to pay a few extra dollars per order.
> *– Mark G., Account Manager, CDWG*

STEP 9

By running an effective internal meeting, you can help ensure activities are properly monitored, numbers are reviewed, and expectations are set. Specify activities for each person in the group, which can be checked and analyzed by everyone in attendance.

To help run an effective meeting, ask yourself:

- Who needs the information you are going to share? Who needs the information firsthand?

- From whom do you need to get firsthand information?
- Who is directly affected by the problem?
- Who can contribute to the achievement of the meeting objectives?
- Who has the authority to approve of a solution or take action?

POINTER

Give them what they want, in the way they want it!

– Art Eyzaguirre, President, ACE Consulting Group, Inc.

Utilizing the previous questions, determine what each person's responsibilities for the meeting will be. Do you need someone to provide specific background information? Do you need someone else to come prepared with suggestions and ideas for discussion? Do you simply need the participants to read a report and be able to discuss it intelligently? Also determine if you need everyone there for the duration of the meeting, or if someone can simply come for part of it. For example, you may only need someone to give a brief presentation of information and then that person can leave.

Whatever you ask of your participants, make sure that you give them a sufficient amount of time to prepare. How many times have you been in a meeting and found that you have information that would have been relevant, but you weren't asked to bring it?

What about meetings with buyers? Running an effective meeting with a buyer is also critical, and the principles outlined above will work well. The goal of any meeting is to be as productive as possible while being as concise as possible.

Know the Sales Culture

Up to this point, everything discussed in this step relates to the concept of sale culture. From the roles you have to play, the way meetings are run, and the way you have to manage your internal organization, sales culture is important. Obviously, you cannot change sales culture by yourself.

Many salespeople have been short lived in the profession because they didn't understand how much the sales culture within an organization could win. It can be extremely frustrating at times when you find that your biggest barrier to success is your own organization—and the possible lack of support that you need to truly succeed.

> **POINTER**
> You have to believe what you are saying, or nobody else ever will.
> – *Tiffany Routon, Human Resources Manager, Industry Intelligence, Inc.*

Just as you often see maps that say "you are here" in order to help you navigate to a destination, this section will serve as your "roadmap" to understanding and navigating five types of sales culture. What does it take to demonstrate and "ratchet up" sales success? Many believe it's as simple as "more activity leads to more success." However, the most successful sales professionals realize that their success ultimately depends on the ability to drive results and that includes *everything*—driving cost reductions in the sales organization, becoming more efficient in the sales position, and ensuring profitability in the buyer–seller relationship, to name but a few.

Culture of Individual Sales Performance

Shown at the bottom of Figure 9.1, the culture of individual sales performance represents the worst-case scenario in alignment and support of your work as sales professional. It doesn't represent a world-class sales organization. This culture is characterized by a lack of organization-wide focus on what it takes to really sell professionally. As result, it's "every person for him or herself" in the sales team. Communication is limited and political savvy is a key element of success. This type of culture creates salespeople who feel they must achieve success on their own. They also feel as if they need to manage the often-misaligned jobs and responsibilities of colleagues who are internally focused instead of market focused. These salespeople are constantly confounded by misaligned processes that seem

FIGURE 9.1

Types of Sales Cultures

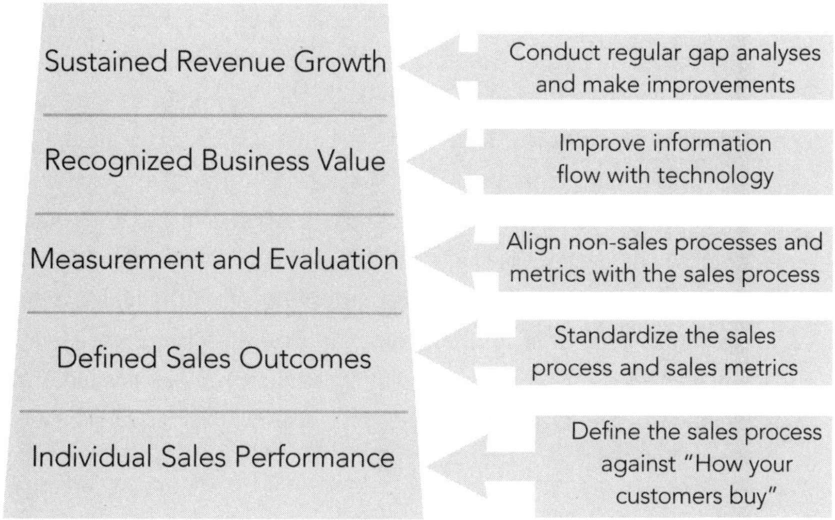

to conflict with sales activity. As a result, the organization appears shortsighted and reactionary, and no foundation is created that builds trust and creates lasting value for customers.

Typical outputs routinely witnessed within this type of sales culture could be identified as (not all-inclusive):

- Pre-purchase expectations are set by sales professionals but not delivered by the organization
- Marketing collateral doesn't align to the sales message
- The salesperson has to retrieve information within the selling organization, often with little support
- The sales professional must correct and manipulate organizational messages to become more relevant.

Key Action Required for Success within this type of selling culture: Define your sales process against how your buyers buy.

STEP 9

Culture of Defined Sales Outcomes

The culture of defined sales outcomes represents organizational alignment and support at its most basic level. The selling organization has instituted many key performance improvements. The organization has established remediation strategies to address internal miscommunication issues, redefine roles and responsibilities, and reset expectations with marketing, sales, customer service, and fulfillment professionals. The organization has also established a relationship management structure to create winning relationships, as well as procedures to quantify customer service, sales, and marketing outcomes. Metrics may not exist to help track outcomes of processes, and mechanisms are in place to detect and address revenue target deviations. The organization has established engagement management processes to request new services as needed and developed benchmarking strategies to constantly assess salesforce competitiveness.

Typical outputs routinely witnessed within this type of culture could be identified as (not all-inclusive):

- Focused sales techniques are utilized by most sales professionals.
- Positive, work-related relationships exist between sales colleagues.
- Rapport and trust exist between sales organization members.
- Documentation is prepared and delivered in a manner that requires little rework by the sales professional.
- Processes and their impact on products or services are assessed.
- Timelines are mostly kept and correspondence is mostly accurate.
- Psychological factors surround the buying–selling relationship.

Key Action Required for Success within this type of selling culture: Standardize the sales process and sales metrics.

STEP 9

Culture of Measurement

The culture of measurement represents a more proactive approach by the organization. The organization has set revenue targets that are reported regularly and utilizes change management processes within a solution-focused selling environment. Escalation management processes are established to address customer service issues and business continuity processes are implemented to ensure superb support of the sales and marketing function to drive revenue. The sales function has standards that are benchmarked against other organizations at least once per year, and business and IT measures are correlated and reported regularly as they pertain to sales efforts.

Typical outputs routinely witnessed within this type of culture could be identified as (not all-inclusive):

- The desired impact to the business is achieved.
- Goods or services are delivered.
- Return-on-investment numbers are met.
- Measurements of success are achieved.
- Project is within scope (if applicable).

Key Action Required for Success within this type of selling culture: Align non-sales processes and metrics with your sales process.

Culture of Recognized Business Value

The culture of recognized business value represents a dedicated and sustained effort to achieve world-class sales excellence. The organization has developed professional standards that align with industry standards, and leverages success stories. The organization is effective in driving costs out of the sales organization while improving business processes and increasing buyer responsiveness. Sales teams meet forecasts and are supported by management processes that have established sales plans. The organization can alert the correct organizations and business units to competitive threats, and sales processes are integrated and mostly automated. The organization has defined and ingrained sales processes that are based on best practices or their equivalent. Single points of weakness are adequately and quickly addressed. A supportive compensation plan is created and implemented and the marketing organization drives market expansion and awareness.

Typical outputs routinely witnessed within this type of culture could be identified as (not all-inclusive):

- Most buyers make renewal or re-buy decisions.
- Up-sell or cross-sell of products or services is easier.
- Buyers are willing to explore the impact the selling organization may have in their organization.
- Creation of strategic partnerships is easier.
- Trust, rapport, and communication flow are more prevalent.

Key Action Required for Success within this type of selling culture: Improving effectiveness and information flow with technology.

Culture of Sustained Revenue Growth

The culture of sustained revenue growth represents a fully capable and aligned sales organization. Repeatable and definable selling processes exist throughout the organization. Supportive processes align to the sales function and are managed in a systematic and holistic way (for example, marketing, sales, and customer service initiatives and efforts). Quantified measures of sales efforts exist. All managers understand what the sales professional needs, how other departments can support him or her, and how their roles as internal stakeholders contribute equally toward an ability to create revenue performance. Learning and best practices exist and are institutionalized. A solid understanding of organizational vision, mission, and goals are thoroughly ingrained through a common language and proper alignment to the customer.

Typical outputs routinely witnessed within this type of culture could be identified as (not all-inclusive):

- All sales goals are accomplished.
- There is proper alignment within the sales organization.

- There is no role ambiguity between sales and marketing functions.
- Sales targets are continuously exceeded.
- A selling cycle management maturity model is leveraged and enhanced with feedback mechanisms adopted.
- At least 70 percent of new proposals are won.
- Technology is leveraged to enable strategic business initiatives.
- Training for sales professionals is provided for continuous improvement opportunities.

POINTER

It's not about you. It's all about your customer and their needs. Take the time to understand how they would use your product or service (it may be different than the last customer), how their company works, how they communicate, and so on. Use this research to build rapport with each customer and make sure they know how important they are.
– Teresa Oswandel, Training Specialist, Deluxe Corporation

Key Action Required for Success within this type of selling culture: Conducting regular gap analyses and making constant improvements.

◆ ◆ ◆

In summary, sales professionals not only have accountability and responsibility for driving revenue, but within the buyer–seller relationship they also play many roles in which they are expected to excel. In this step, sales professionals need to maximize their time investment and effectively run productive meetings and skillfully maneuver within the sales culture of the organization. The last step in the process highlights how the most successful sales professionals are passionate about lifelong learning and never rest on their current laurels or skills—instead they constantly focus on improving themselves and developing competencies.

WORKSHEET 9.1

Worksheet Running Effective Meetings

Instructions: Use this worksheet to ensure that your meetings are productive, valuable, and have all of the key players required in attendance. You may find you don't even need to call a meeting!

Do You Need to Have a Meeting?

Answer the following questions to determine if a meeting is your best option.

• Can you clearly state the purpose of your meeting?	☐ Yes ☐ No
• Do you want input from others to solve a problem, plan a project, or brainstorm?	☐ Yes ☐ No
• Are you going to act on participants' input?	☐ Yes ☐ No
• Do you need to deliver information to a lot of people but don't want to write it?	☐ Yes ☐ No
• Do you want to motivate and energize a team?	☐ Yes ☐ No

If you answered "no" to one or more questions, you probably do not need to call a meeting. Consider making phone calls or sending emails or a memo. If you do need to call a meeting, list the key goals of the meeting below:

-
-
-
-
-
-
-

STEP 9

Worksheet 9.1, continued

Who Needs to Attend?

Considering what you want to achieve with your meeting, who can make contributions to its success? Who needs to come? List the names of the people you are considering, and then note the reason that person should attend.

Name	Reason to Attend

Tip! If you can't think of a good reason for someone to attend, you should probably cross him or her off the list. For optimum efficiency, you probably don't want more than six people to attend, but that depends somewhat on the kind of meeting you are planning.

Who Needs to Do What?

Now that you have decided whom to invite to the meeting, determine if you need someone to carry out any specific tasks in the meeting, such as presenting information or coming up with preliminary ideas. Also identify whom you want to carry out the roles of timekeeper, facilitator, and notetaker.

Name	Task or Role

continued on next page

What Facilities/Equipment Are Needed?

To identify the facilities and equipment you might need, answer the following questions:

- Do you have a space that's big enough to comfortably accommodate all the participants?

- Do you need any special seating arrangements?

- Is the meeting going to take long enough to require breaks or refreshments? Should you go off site?

- How are you planning to deliver information or have notes taken?

- Is the equipment that you need to deliver information available in the room or facilities that you have chosen?

What Needs to Get Done?

The last component in planning your meeting is determining what is going to happen. To identify the right agenda items in the right quantity (not too many, not too few), answer the following questions:

- What has to happen to accomplish your objective?

- What is the most important outcome you want from the meeting?

- If meeting time were cut in half for some reason, what would be the first thing removed from the agenda?

- If this is a follow-up meeting, what agenda items left from the last meeting should be taken care of?

- During which activity are meeting participants going to commit to further action and next steps?

- Are there any minor issues that could be quickly cleared up during this meeting?

Worksheet 9.1, continued

Activities

Now, list the activities. Mark each activity high priority (H) or low (L). Keep low-priority items on the agenda, but use the priorities as a guide to estimate the time required for each item. If possible, go through high-priority activities first both to capitalize on the energy of the group and to ensure that they are addressed.

Activity	Priority
1.	☐ High ☐ Low
2.	☐ High ☐ Low
3.	☐ High ☐ Low
4.	☐ High ☐ Low
5.	☐ High ☐ Low
6.	☐ High ☐ Low
7.	☐ High ☐ Low
8.	☐ High ☐ Low
9.	☐ High ☐ Low
10.	☐ High ☐ Low

STEP 9

NOTES

STEP TEN

Develop World-Class Competencies

OVERVIEW

- Leverage competency
- World-class sales professionalism
- Foundational competencies
- Create and close opportunities
- Protect accounts

Think about any new job you've started. You were probably given basic objectives that you were expected to achieve or a vague description of the skills you needed—but without a clear definition of how you were going to be evaluated, how success would be measured, or even how to get started.

For example, as a new sales professional, you may be asked to

- drive revenue
- create and maintain successful client relationships
- build trust and loyalty with every client interaction
- capture more market share and competitive knowledge
- execute the vision and strategy of the management team
- follow the sales process
- maintain an accurate forecast.

While these goals are important, they don't necessarily set a clear path toward defining what you need to know and what you need to do to accomplish them. Think about it—within each of these objectives you could know about the

- selling skills required
- product or service you are selling
- trends and changes in the industries you serve
- company-specific steps to take to get something done
- management of resources, technology, and people.

Even if you know all of these things (and it is a lot to know), what do you need to actually do? Put another way—even if you know what to sell, do you know how to sell it? If you know what expectation to set, do you know how to set it? If you know what makes a great presentation, do you know how to give it?

It doesn't stop there. Even if you understand what you need to know and what you need to do to be successful, how do you build five years of experience, and not just one year of experience five times? How do you continuously improve, learn, and become more trusted over time?

Leverage Competence

The next competitive advantage in selling is competency. Competency will set you apart as a trusted advisor. And competencies are the basic building block of professionalism. Competencies are defined by the American Society for Training and Development (ASTD) as the clusters of skills, knowledge, abilities, and behaviors required for job success. As an effective and efficient trusted advisor, you can use competencies to direct your own success on the job. You can also use competencies to guide your personal training and development, as well as that of your fellow sales team members.

Often, competencies can be organized into a "competency model," which is a visual representation of the competencies required for success in a specific job or profession. A competency-modeling approach is unique in that it statistically validates and identifies important and relevant knowledge and skills.

Why a Competency-Based Approach?

All sales team members, not just quota-carrying sales professionals, have a key stake in sales performance. To create sustained revenue performance all sales team members must take more accountability and responsibility for sales results, no matter how long they have been with the organization. That means you must do your part in order to become a key contributor.

Why? Because great sales professionals are willing and able to analyze their own performance gaps, choose appropriate professional development solutions, and evaluate their personal effectiveness. A competency-based approach can provide a guideline for this continuous improvement process. To help, a statistically validated competency model can guide you through your own personal development by

- **Synchronizing to the customer's buying process**—A competency-based approach can identify many competencies that help sales team members maintain proper emphasis on the crucial buyer–seller relationship. This helps you assess every buyer interaction and determine the most appropriate activity to help facilitate buyer decision making.
- **Employing improved time management skills**—A competency-based approach helps sales team members determine the most appropriate course of action when planning their daily, weekly, or monthly activities through more clearly defined role expectations. Armed with a more solid understanding of the roles they play, you can balance the demands placed on their time from multiple stakeholders who often have conflicting interests.
- **Practicing continuous personal improvement**—A competency-based approach can help you take a proactive, continuous-improvement approach to personal development and your ability to manage the sales process, leverage technology, and share knowledge internally and externally.
- **Increasing personal influence**—A competency-based approach can help sales team members identify the competencies required to create and build influence with their

customers. Each of the foundational competencies provides a detailed breakdown of the critical elements for building the kind of influence you need to effectively manage, direct, and advise your customers.

A competency-based approach can also provide a common language by which to facilitate communication across departmental boundaries. For example, by referring to the roles, competencies, and outputs of the sales profession, sales managers across departments can share a common language and work together to effect change by

- **Selecting the right sales organization members**—A competency-based approach can help you assess the sales organization against a definition of world class during the interview process. Because many organizations focus on cultural fit and an assessment of what is required to sell in their organization, you can determine fit by clearly understanding the organization's support of the sales team (development, operations, management, and compensation) found within the model.
- **Analyzing and coaching performance**—A competency-based approach can create a simple model for troubleshooting performance problems in the sales system or for planning solutions to improve performance. When you become familiar with the model, you can become an internal consultant, and become more adept at identifying problems, approaching salespeople, and delivering coaching.
- **Choosing learning solutions, managing change, and evaluating results**—A competency-based approach suggests many causes for sales team performance gaps and identifies possible solutions for change. By becoming an expert at understanding the model, sales managers will learn to choose appropriate training solutions, manage change, and evaluate results.
- **Clearly defining expectations**—A competency-based approach helps sales managers define what is expected of team members within the sales system. By focusing on the

entire selling system and the key players within it, sales managers can ensure they provide clear guidance, make appropriate changes, and provide coaching that addresses any confusion within the system.

- **Coaching for improved performance**—A competency-based approach can help sales managers better understand their team members. The approach offers a validated dictionary of competencies that can be honed through one-on-one discussions that help motivate, change behavior, and improve focus.

Wouldn't it be great to have your management team provide you this support? If it's not, now's your chance to have a coaching conversation!

World-Class Sales Professionalism

Lucky for you, a full competency model for the sales profession was published in 2009 by ASTD in *World-Class Selling: New Sales Competencies* (2009). In this book, more than 2,500 professionals contributed to the creation of 450 competencies, outputs, and behaviors. Collectively, these statements were identified and presented in a model to help individuals build professional selling knowledge and skill.

The model was created by sales professionals, for sales professionals. The lasting value of the model is ensured by its broad perspective: it defines the way people operate within the sales system, whether they are directly responsible for revenue generation or support those who are, rather than speaking from a narrow, transaction-based approach. It assumes—and celebrates—the fact that anyone who works within the sales

POINTER

Find a mentor. Someone who knows the product inside and out. Talk with them about the product and how they sell. Have them copy you on sales emails and learn the success language they use. Capture the passion they have when selling the product.
– Lorrie T. Carter, RN/Sales Rep, August Systems, Inc.

team is a part of its success and, as such, deserves intentional, focused professional development to ensure his or her own success.

The World-Class Sales Competency Model presented in Figure 10.1 can help you understand what it takes to create and close opportunities, manage accounts, protect accounts, set sales strategy, and much more.

Foundational Competencies

World-Class Selling: New Sales Competencies also identified 29 foundational competencies as common, core, and critical to all sales professionals, regardless of job title or role. These 29 foundational competencies cluster into four categories in the pyramid shown in Figure 10.1. These logical groupings help sales team members define and assess their level of competence.

Partnering Competencies

Partnering competencies enable the effective creation and leveraging of relationships within the sales context and facilitate sales interactions. This cluster includes

- aligning to customers
- building relationships
- communicating effectively
- negotiating positions
- setting expectations
- spanning boundaries.

Insight Competencies

Insight competencies enable the development of robust analysis and synthesis skills. They permit sales team members to use information effectively and efficiently. This cluster includes

- analyzing capacity
- building a business case

FIGURE 10.1

The ASTD World-Class Sales Competency Model

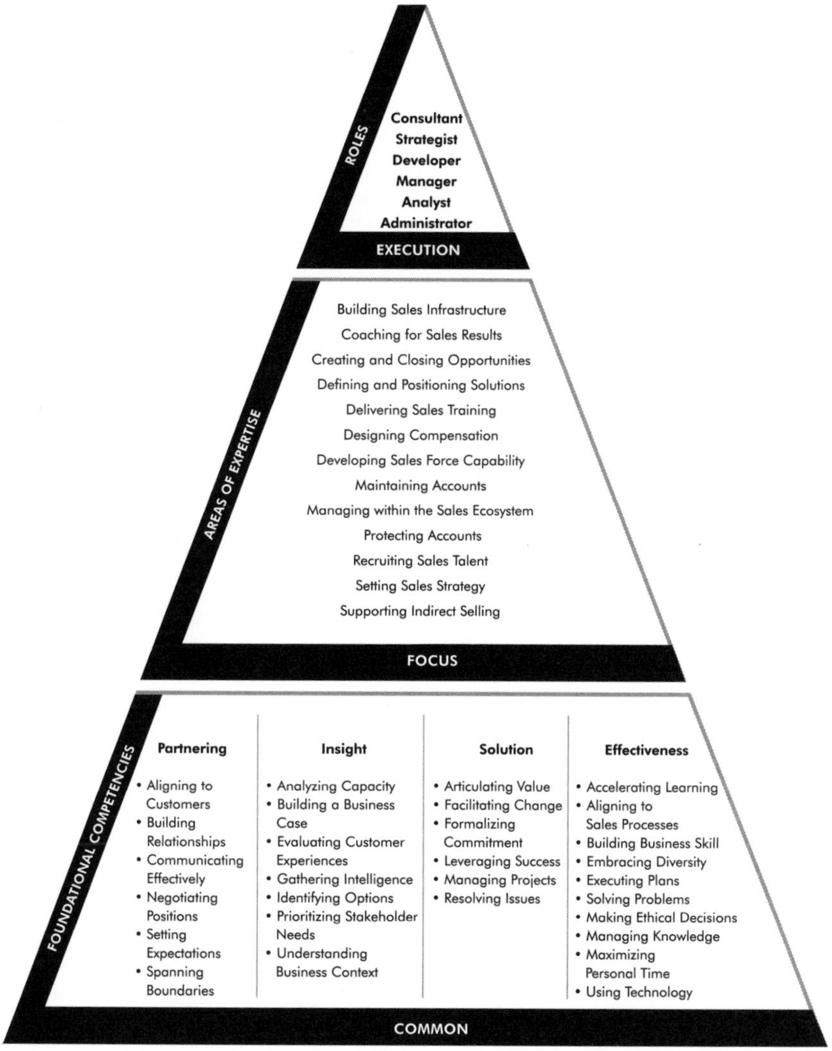

STEP 10

- evaluating customer experiences
- gathering intelligence
- identifying options
- prioritizing stakeholder needs
- understanding the business context.

Solution Competencies

Solution competencies enable the effective development of strategies and generation of support for the resulting solutions. This cluster includes

- articulating value
- facilitating change
- formalizing agreements
- leveraging success
- managing projects
- resolving issues.

Effectiveness Competencies

Effectiveness competencies enable the demonstration and development of personal effectiveness and responsibility. This cluster includes

- accelerating learning
- aligning to the sales process
- building business skills
- embracing diversity
- executing plans
- solving problems
- making ethical decisions
- managing knowledge
- maximizing personal time
- using technology.

To help you objectively analyze where you are with regard to specific competencies for the sales profession, complete the worksheet beginning on page 190.

Create and Close Opportunities

Let's look at what the model instructs you to do in order to create and close opportunities. According to the World-Class Sales Competency Model, you must

- continuously scan for prospects in order to achieve new sales
- expand account control and populate account pipeline
- leverage customer referrals and target new leads
- follow up on leads and assess prospect readiness to buy
- perform interest-building calls as necessary
- build and drive opportunities by generating and nurturing internal and external stakeholder interest
- manage sales cycle progress
- conduct or orchestrate business or technical qualifications
- acquire the technical expertise required for well-targeted solution design, business case justification, and subsequent negotiations
- drive or manage the resources necessary for effective negotiations, including the alignment of expert input within the negotiation strategy
- ask for the business, effectively address any objections or concerns, close unique transactions, and achieve a mutually beneficial win for the buyer and seller.

POINTER

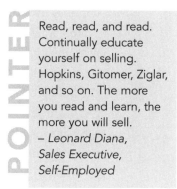

Read, read, and read. Continually educate yourself on selling. Hopkins, Gitomer, Ziglar, and so on. The more you read and learn, the more you will sell.
– Leonard Diana, Sales Executive, Self-Employed

The World-Class Sales Competency Model shows that sales professionals who are trusted advisors not only accomplish these actions when creating and closing opportunities, they also

- **Research and target prospects**—Actively research available sources to identify likely prospects based on alignment to product or service markets, known business needs, typical customer profiles, business activities, competitive market position, customer challenges, product or service spend, and competitive presence in account; review prospects and determine where or how to allocate efforts and resources; develop an approach strategy tailored to the most appropriate individuals who have decision-making authority.

- **Conduct interest building calls (cold calls) when applicable**—Appropriately manage customer prospecting to connect directly with future customers while not alienating them; generate immediate, compelling customer interest in the selling organization, ensure its product or service offers sufficient value to generate a willingness to continue the sales dialogue; and initiate exploratory discussions in order to schedule solid and specific follow-up sales calls in an effort to continue facilitating buying processes.
- **Identify, follow up, and manage sales leads**—Build reciprocal lead-sharing networks in order to build the sales funnel with prospective clients, and act on any new lead in a timely manner in order to capitalize on interest and compelling needs.
- **Gain interest**—Leverage marketing materials to stimulate client interest; explore client curiosity from various perspectives (business, financial, market) to capture key variables and contingencies in order to nurture opportunities; generate customer interest through discussion of potential benefits; and actively shape components of each opportunity to reflect client priorities and adequately address client needs.
- **Qualify opportunities**—Assess client operations and business position for potential partnering opportunities; assess client balance sheet and business health to determine feasibility of partnering; identify and align required resources for pursuit and future solution deployment; determine scope and nature of risk as a necessary input to developing appropriate pricing and risk management strategies; and determine or orchestrate identification of opportunities and assess requirements for third-party involvement.

- **Develop winning proposals**—Develop compelling value propositions aligned with customer needs, business priorities, and/or technical and operational requirements; orchestrate and align the contributions of functional and technical experts; communicate key competitive advantages; work with others to ensure appropriate pricing; and manage the milestones essential for timely proposal delivery.

> **POINTER**
> Read one new business book each quarter. This simple activity builds business acumen and sparks creativity that will show up in every customer interaction.
> *– Jill Myrick, Owner, Meeting to Win, LLC*

- **Build business justification cases**—Collaborate with financial, legal, and technical experts to develop a business justification for each specific opportunity in order to ensure internal buy-in; enlist champions within both buyer and seller organizations; work with internal stakeholders to customize the opportunity to internal requirements while avoiding compromises that might threaten client acceptance or solution integrity; and identify and communicate all risks associated with the opportunity and address these challenges with solution contingencies or fall-back positions.
- **Orchestrate support for negotiations**—Where warranted, coordinate the input of legal, technical, and financial experts seamlessly into the development of a negotiation strategy; ensure that stakeholders understand their role in negotiation; focus efforts of others on achieving the business outcome; continuously check with experts to ensure commitments are valid and can be delivered; and drive to close and ask for the business at appropriate time.
- **Maintain opportunity momentum to expand sales**—Capitalize on early wins and customer satisfaction in order to expand business wider and deeper into the account.

Competencies of Top Sales Performers

People want to do well. Most people in an occupation usually try to become the best they can. According to Hickman and Lewis, to do this, people must first start with an objective analysis of where they currently are and where they want to be.

While selling is a science, the good news is that professionals who succeed in sales have traits and competencies that can be acquired. Most professionals who achieve high-level sales positions actively work toward gaining job-specific knowledge and skills. These are the "must haves"—the nonnegotiable characteristics that most sales managers are looking for when hiring top-notch sales professionals.

Protect Accounts

According to the World-Class Sales Competency Model, to create and close opportunities, you must

- gather account intelligence and maintain current understanding of customer's business
- develop and monitor sales plans
- monitor and communicate sales forecasts and pipeline activities to ensure accuracy
- develop expanded relationships with customers to achieve trusted advisor status and entry into business planning activities
- screen account activities and protect customers from unnecessary sales or marketing activities
- monitor competitive growth in accounts and build strategies for countering competitive messages
- where warranted, determine account transition readiness to sales "farming," and maintain customer trust during and following this transition
- ensure customer satisfaction as well as delivery or deployment alignment to contractual terms and conditions.

Sales professionals who are trusted advisors not only accomplish the actions above when protecting accounts, they also

- **Gather and monitor account intelligence**—Maintain account business direction in a manner consistent with client needs; establish networks in customer business in order to stay abreast of current or emerging requirements; and scan relevant external publications or websites for account-related business information.
- **Document account plan and sales forecasts**—Develop strategies and plans for managing account pursuit activities; assess activities to plan; prioritize and coordinate opportunity pursuits across multiple accounts to maintain a healthy sales funnel; and develop, communicate, and monitor sales forecasts to ensure accuracy.
- **Build client executive business relationships**—Widen the breadth and depth of account penetration to achieve exposure to business planning; use professional presence to frame selling messages in terms of client's business (rather than operational or technical) benefits; incorporate key business and financial metrics into sales positioning messages; demonstrate comfort at various business levels and possess the social skills necessary for interacting effectively with senior-level executives; and position the company represented and the benefits of partnering as the essential components of the business relationship desired as opposed to focusing on more purely transactional relationship.
- **Cultivate and develop trusted advisor status**—Ensure that product or service value propositions align and resonate with customer needs; provide on-demand consultative advice; check

> **POINTER**
>
> Humility finds itself to be a positive trait in many aspects of one's approach to business allowing one to be comfortable being uncomfortable, thus, transcending what is known today and resulting in deeper knowledge tomorrow.
> *– Steve W. Korinek, VP Sales and Marketing, The Jacob Group*

STEP 10

the accuracy and utility of recommendations prior to their communication and avoid making inaccurate claims; conduct oneself professionally in all customer communications and interactions with discreetness and confidentiality when required; and credit competitive claims where warranted to maintain credibility and trust.

- **Protect and expand accounts**—Ensure that all contractual deployment or fulfillment obligations are met and customer satisfaction is achieved; monitor account activity to minimize rogue selling and disruptive marketing; generally maintain overall account focal point leadership; and monitor competitive activities in accounts and appropriately counter competitive messages while blocking future competitor inroads.
- **Manage deployment readiness and resource alignment**—Ensure accurate understanding of requirements derived from closed opportunities (such as terms and conditions and service-level agreements) and ensure knowledge is dispersed among personnel engaged in post-sale activity (fulfillment, delivery, and so on); where warranted, act as the focal point for deal education and preparation within individual geographies; and, where required, facilitate the resource troubleshooting essential for successfully launching complex initiatives.

Sales professionals should also produce the following outputs as they protect accounts:

- strategic account plan
- sales funnel
- customer checkups
- forecast updates
- sales forecasts
- marketing feedback
- executive-level communications
- portfolio and client reviews
- account profiles
- service-level agreements

- legal documentation
- management and team member updates
- industry and competitive position papers
- competitive analyses
- transition plans
- company-specific paperwork
- solution roadmap.

◆ ◆ ◆

This step focused on the final capstone needed on your path to becoming a successful sales professional—investing in your long-term personal development by understanding the common and critical competencies required and how to achieve them. If you are truly serious about being a world-class sales professional, you'll invest in your personal development, accept failures as learning opportunities, and leverage the sage wisdom, tips, and 10 steps outlined in this book to help guide you on your journey.

WORKSHEET 10.1

Assess Your Competencies

Instructions: The first step in learning is to become aware that a gap exists in our knowledge and skills. Without this awareness, it's impossible to seek out understanding. Sometimes awareness comes from external events, such as losing business or being told of the deficiency. For any sales professional, becoming aware of areas where you could improve is, at times, hard to swallow.

Use this worksheet to assess, prioritize, and plan your actions for learning and develop a personalized professional development plan for yourself. Each of the statements below can be assessed and objectively measured by you, your colleagues, and your supervisor. Make multiple copies to gather feedback from others.

Name: ______________________________ Date: _________________________

Use the following proficiency scale to place an "X" in the appropriate box to represent your level of proficiency as defined below

1 = No to Little Proficiency: At best, understands the concepts and language of the topic

2 = Limited Proficiency: Possesses a working knowledge but still needs help

3 = Consistent Proficiency: Able to perform without help from others or job aids

4 = Advanced Proficiency: Able to consistently solve unique and difficult problems

5 = Exceptional Proficiency: In addition to consistent high performance, possesses the ability to teach others about the topic

Partnering Competencies. These competencies enable the effective creation and leveraging of relationships within the sales context and facilitate sales interactions.

Partnering Competency: Spanning Boundaries					
How well do you:	Proficiency 1	2	3	4	5
• Build positive, collaborative relationships across organizations to minimize conflict and ensure a common focus	☐	☐	☐	☐	☐
• Where responsibility is ambiguous, take ownership for what needs to be done to achieve success	☐	☐	☐	☐	☐

STEP 10

Partnering Competency: Communicating Effectively					
How well do you:	Proficiency 1	2	3	4	5
• Closely attend to what is said and ask for clarification if needed to ensure accurate understanding	☐	☐	☐	☐	☐
• Communicate written or verbal messages clearly, concisely, accurately, and persuasively	☐	☐	☐	☐	☐
• Respond quickly to the information or assistance requests from others	☐	☐	☐	☐	☐
• Effectively use persuasion to achieve desired outcomes	☐	☐	☐	☐	☐

Partnering Competency: Aligning to Customers					
How well do you:	Proficiency 1	2	3	4	5
• Contribute to customer satisfaction by establishing enduring relationships built on trust and responsiveness	☐	☐	☐	☐	☐
• Represent the customer's interest in company business planning and decision making	☐	☐	☐	☐	☐

Partnering Competency: Setting Expectations					
How well do you:	Proficiency 1	2	3	4	5
• Effectively communicate and align stakeholders to program or project expectations	☐	☐	☐	☐	☐
• Communicate responsibilities to others in a way that clearly differentiates who is responsible for what, when, and to what standard	☐	☐	☐	☐	☐
• Understand and address potential obstacles to proposed solutions	☐	☐	☐	☐	☐

continued on next page

Worksheet 10.1, continued

Partnering Competency: Negotiating Positions					
How well do you:	Proficiency 1	2	3	4	5
• Develop thorough negotiation strategies that include both optimum and fall-back positions	☐	☐	☐	☐	☐
• Clarify a position or, when necessary, use experts to handle stakeholder objections and ensure accurate understanding	☐	☐	☐	☐	☐
• Build commitment to agreements and buy-in among stakeholders for moving forward	☐	☐	☐	☐	☐

Partnering Competency: Building Relationships					
How well do you:	Proficiency 1	2	3	4	5
• Build positive, professional relationships with others at all levels of an organization	☐	☐	☐	☐	☐
• Develop relationships to deeper levels of trust and confidence	☐	☐	☐	☐	☐

Insight Competencies. These competencies enable the development of robust analysis and synthesis skills.

Insight Competency: Analyzing Organizational Capacity					
How well do you:	Proficiency 1	2	3	4	5
• Accurately identify the type and quantity of resources needed to achieve results	☐	☐	☐	☐	☐
• Balance risk with benefits to identify the best path forward	☐	☐	☐	☐	☐

STEP 10

Insight Competency: Understanding the Business Context					
How well do you:	Proficiency 1	2	3	4	5
• Understand how one's work relates to the work of others	☐	☐	☐	☐	☐
• Understand at a level appropriate to one's responsibilities	☐	☐	☐	☐	☐

Insight Competency: Evaluating Customer Experiences					
Key Actions and Behaviors:	Proficiency 1	2	3	4	5
• Evaluate customer experience with solutions to resolve challenges and ensure successful implementation	☐	☐	☐	☐	☐
• Communicate the benefits of a solution using business or organizational metrics valued and understood by stakeholders	☐	☐	☐	☐	☐

Insight Competency: Gathering Intelligence					
Key Actions and Behaviors:	Proficiency 1	2	3	4	5
• Determine the range, type, and scope of information needed to address a problem or opportunity	☐	☐	☐	☐	☐
• Apply the most appropriate tools and strategies to gather needed information	☐	☐	☐	☐	☐
• Develop multiple information sources to maintain the quality and validity of data collection over time	☐	☐	☐	☐	☐

continued on next page

Insight Competency: Prioritizing Stakeholder Needs					
Key Actions and Behaviors:	Proficiency 1	2	3	4	5
• Thoroughly diagnose needs to identify their true nature	☐	☐	☐	☐	☐
• Assess and prioritize needs as the basis for guiding planning	☐	☐	☐	☐	☐

Insight Competency: Identifying Options					
Key Actions and Behaviors:	Proficiency 1	2	3	4	5
• Critically explore and assess the range of possible solutions as input to decision making	☐	☐	☐	☐	☐
• Resist premature closure and keep options open to ensure selection of the most appropriate alternatives	☐	☐	☐	☐	☐
• Assess the impact of all alternatives as a basis for selecting and prioritizing the best option	☐	☐	☐	☐	☐
• Commit to a course of action after carefully weighing the consequences of each alternative	☐	☐	☐	☐	☐

Insight Competency: Building a Business Case					
Key Actions and Behaviors:	Proficiency 1	2	3	4	5
• Work with stakeholders to identify the most relevant business or operational metrics upon which to build a case	☐	☐	☐	☐	☐
• Build a case to justify the commitment of resources to an initiative	☐	☐	☐	☐	☐
• Clearly identify the business/financial benefits to be realized by investments	☐	☐	☐	☐	☐

Worksheet 10.1, continued

Solution Competencies. These competencies enable the effective development of strategies and generation of support for the resulting solutions.

Solution Competency: Facilitating Change

Key Actions and Behaviors:	Proficiency 1	2	3	4	5
◆ Advocate for change and its benefits to facilitate change initiatives	☐	☐	☐	☐	☐
◆ Manage work to ensure that it aligns to changing requirements	☐	☐	☐	☐	☐
◆ Look for opportunities to improve the organization's work practices and attitudes	☐	☐	☐	☐	☐

Solution Competency: Formalizing Agreements

Key Actions and Behaviors:	Proficiency 1	2	3	4	5
◆ Fulfill project commitments in a way that builds and maintains stakeholder confidence and support over the project life cycle	☐	☐	☐	☐	☐
◆ Communicate agreements in a timely manner to expedite execution	☐	☐	☐	☐	☐
◆ Document agreements to ensure clear, accurate, and mutual understanding of expectations among all stakeholders	☐	☐	☐	☐	☐

Solution Competency: Resolving Issues

Key Actions and Behaviors:	Proficiency 1	2	3	4	5
◆ Develop contingency plans and monitor situations for issues requiring their use	☐	☐	☐	☐	☐
◆ Monitor implementation/development to ensure success	☐	☐	☐	☐	☐
◆ Resolve problems through personal intervention or escalation to more appropriate resources	☐	☐	☐	☐	☐

continued on next page

Solution Competency: Managing Projects

Key Actions and Behaviors:	Proficiency 1	2	3	4	5
• Organize and manage projects systematically to ensure the quality of the deliverable and the achievement of milestones	☐	☐	☐	☐	☐
• Manage project resources efficiently and effectively to ensure cost-effective results	☐	☐	☐	☐	☐
• Adapt project strategies, methods, and resources to shifting requirements	☐	☐	☐	☐	☐

Solution Competency: Leveraging Success

Key Actions and Behaviors:	Proficiency 1	2	3	4	5
• Build on success to expand both business relationships and mutually beneficial opportunities	☐	☐	☐	☐	☐
• Document and communicate best practices	☐	☐	☐	☐	☐

Solution Competency: Articulating Value

Key Actions and Behaviors:	Proficiency 1	2	3	4	5
• Ensure that the value of a solution incorporates stakeholder priorities	☐	☐	☐	☐	☐
• Craft value propositions in a way that resonates with the needs of all stakeholders	☐	☐	☐	☐	☐
• Confirm the validity of the proposed solution with all stakeholders to ensure its acceptance	☐	☐	☐	☐	☐

Effectiveness Competencies. These competencies enable the demonstration and development of personal effectiveness and responsibility

Effectiveness Competency: Building Business Skills					
Key Actions and Behaviors:	Proficiency 1	2	3	4	5
◆ Incorporate understanding of business and industry factors important to stakeholders into work	☐	☐	☐	☐	☐
◆ Use business insights to improve personal contributions to the organization	☐	☐	☐	☐	☐
◆ Use understanding of contracts and statements of work to define and organize work	☐	☐	☐	☐	☐
◆ Apply financial understanding to the prudent use of company resources	☐	☐	☐	☐	☐

Effectiveness Competency: Solving Problems					
Key Actions and Behaviors:	Proficiency 1	2	3	4	5
◆ Approach challenges creatively and from a fresh perspective	☐	☐	☐	☐	☐
◆ Resist habitual ways of thinking and actively integrate whatever approaches will solve a problem	☐	☐	☐	☐	☐

Effectiveness Competency: Embracing Diversity					
Key Actions and Behaviors:	Proficiency 1	2	3	4	5
◆ Demonstrate respect for others	☐	☐	☐	☐	☐
◆ Value diverse perspectives and seek to learn from those with different backgrounds	☐	☐	☐	☐	☐
◆ Use the varied experiences of others to stimulate creativity and innovation	☐	☐	☐	☐	☐

continued on next page

Worksheet 10.1, continued

Effectiveness Competency: Making Ethical Decisions					
Key Actions and Behaviors:	Proficiency 1	2	3	4	5
• Demonstrate personal integrity in honoring obligations and performing as a trustworthy employee	☐	☐	☐	☐	☐
• Incorporate quality considerations into decision making	☐	☐	☐	☐	☐

Effectiveness Competency: Managing Knowledge					
Key Actions and Behaviors:	Proficiency 1	2	3	4	5
• Actively and openly share information and knowledge with others	☐	☐	☐	☐	☐
• Remove obstacles to the flow of information and advocate tools and processes that facilitate the ease of information storage and retrieval	☐	☐	☐	☐	☐

Effectiveness Competency: Using Technology					
Key Actions and Behaviors:	Proficiency 1	2	3	4	5
• Maintain understanding of the technical innovations that contribute to more efficient and effective work	☐	☐	☐	☐	☐
• Use information technology to align and expedite work	☐	☐	☐	☐	☐
• Actively seek out and use new technology that will contribute to personal growth and benefit the company	☐	☐	☐	☐	☐

Effectiveness Competency: Accelerating Learning					
Key Actions and Behaviors:	Proficiency 1	2	3	4	5
◆ Take responsibility for personal learning and development	☐	☐	☐	☐	☐
◆ Take full advantage of all available learning options to achieve personal development objectives	☐	☐	☐	☐	☐
◆ Seek out feedback and information to develop or change behavior	☐	☐	☐	☐	☐

Effectiveness Competency: Executing Plans					
Key Actions and Behaviors:	Proficiency 1	2	3	4	5
◆ Develop plans that clearly communicate the activities needed to implement a strategy	☐	☐	☐	☐	☐
◆ Build enthusiasm and commitment to a plan of action	☐	☐	☐	☐	☐
◆ Use plans to guide action while adapting them as needed to changing requirements	☐	☐	☐	☐	☐
◆ Deliver to commitments in compliance with budget, time, and quality expectations	☐	☐	☐	☐	☐

Effectiveness Competency: Maximizing Personal Time					
Key Actions and Behaviors:	Proficiency 1	2	3	4	5
◆ Incorporate a strategic perspective in activity planning	☐	☐	☐	☐	☐
◆ Apply appropriate time management techniques to focus, prioritize, and track tasks	☐	☐	☐	☐	☐

continued on next page

Worksheet 10.1, continued

Effectiveness Competency: Aligning to the Sales Process					
Key Actions and Behaviors:	Proficiency 1	2	3	4	5
• Align and relate work to sales success	☐	☐	☐	☐	☐
• Value customer satisfaction and treat recipients of his or her work as a "customer"	☐	☐	☐	☐	☐
• Understand buying/selling processes and use that understanding to facilitate personalization and customization of sales solutions	☐	☐	☐	☐	☐
• Ensure that work helps to advance sales	☐	☐	☐	☐	☐

STEP 10

Conclusion

Many would argue that the only competitive advantage an organization possesses is its people. As a result, it's the people who are the key enablers of an organization's ability to position itself successfully in the market. To succeed in the market, most organizations have to bring in revenue. Therefore, nothing happens in business unless someone sells something. To sell something in today's business environment, you have to be a true knowledge worker, able to operate within a complex system of conversation, communication, and information. You must be able to take data, turn it into information, and eventually shape and wield it as knowledge that is relevant, timely, and tailored to your buyer, which requires skill and talent. It is this skill and talent that helps you become a trusted advisor.

Sales professionals are effective and efficient trusted advisors, who can earn a buyer's trust, build relationships, and give effective advice about specific business challenges. To become a trusted advisor, you must be able to work smart and work hard. You must be able to think on your feet, be creative, and make ethical business decisions, and you have to be a business problem solver. These skills are absolutely crucial in today's business environment.

You must also have the ability to grasp your organization's vision, mission, and solutions and somehow form a value proposition into a repeatable, measurable, and adaptable process that builds trust with a buyer. Your ability to competitively position is crucial in any selling situation. Since you are the closest to the point of sale, you have a unique chance to influence buyer perceptions, especially in a one-on-one setting.

The game of selling is changing. Both buyers and sellers have different tactics they apply regarding the rules, strategies, and methods. By understanding the playing field in this manner, you can develop a personal selling process that will help you succeed. Just as a sporting event progresses through a series of periods (or quarters), your personal sales process can progress through a set of stages that help you assess how well you are doing. Likewise, as the players in a sports game rely on the condition of the playing surface in order to complete the game effectively, you must understand the support and alignment of your selling organization.

However, in this game there are no winners or losers, per se. Instead, both you and your buyers work together to collaboratively create the game. You can work together as one team to beat the business problem being addressed. This is the impact of selling—to collaborate with buyers to create a solution together.

To reach this level of cocreation, you have to be trusted and credible. Trust is based on your reputation. Trust comes from your customers' experiences with you over time, from knowledge that what you say is true and in their best interests. If you want the customers' trust, you have to earn it because it is built on honesty and an obvious commitment to your customers and the success of their businesses—they are relying on you to help them achieve their goals. Oftentimes, the fate of their jobs will rest in the decision to trust you. From an ethical perspective, then, the establishment of trust between you and your customer precludes any form of dishonesty, even those seemingly harmless "white lies" used to save face or avoid uncomfortable or embarrassing situations.

Credibility comes from performance, not talk. It means possessing and displaying a belief in your company, its products, and the way it does business. It means having a thorough knowledge of your products and their applications, and showing a willingness to learn about your customers and their unique problems and needs. Credibility comes from a track record of successes and an ability to apply the lessons learned. It's at the heart of true professionalism. Like trust, credibility takes time to build and depends heavily on your professional reputation.

Good Selling!

APPENDIX A

Introduction to the World of Selling

What would you guess keeps most CEOs of for-profit organizations up at night? Growing a company's revenue and profits, of course! The driving force behind accomplishing this mission-critical goal involves selling—that is, structuring, negotiating, and closing smart business deals that create a win–win situation for both the customer and the selling organization.

Think about it: Nothing happens in most companies unless a sale is made. Whether you are currently in sales or trying to land your first job in the profession, selling professionals have a mission-critical role to "drive revenue," which in turn enables growth for a company.

> **Accountability and Responsibility in Selling**
>
> All business owners want more revenue, and they often need more skilled and experienced sales professionals to accomplish that goal. Accountability and responsibility are two traits required to be a great sales professional. As such, sales professionals must embrace these traits and ensure that they clearly understand how their performance will be monitored and measured.
>
> Think about the equation to calculate profit. The first part of the equation is "revenue."
>
> Revenue – Expenses = Profits (and enables growth)

Stockholders invest in an organization because they expect dividends and more shareholder value in return for their investment. If the selling organization does not hit its target revenue number, or if the deals landed are structured poorly and do not net the target profit numbers, then the company shrinks and employees often lose their jobs.

With so much riding on the success of the sales organization within a company, sales professionals are accountable and responsible for everything from initial prospecting to closing a sale to ultimately hitting the magic "quota" number that measures success.

In short, the profession of selling is extremely complex; don't let anyone tell you otherwise. Individuals who have been in the sales profession for any length of time will confirm how complex it really is. At the same time, most people in the business world (who do not sell) would readily admit that they would experience difficulties in selling to another person or organization. Despite the complexity of the sales profession and the high level of knowledge and skill needed to succeed, people don't exactly look up to, or respect, salespeople and business executives.

In a 2008 Gallup Poll survey conducted by CNN, several job titles related to selling were found to be the least trustworthy as compared with other job titles. In fact, the lowest rated occupations for honesty and ethics included many job titles linked to selling, such as business executives, stockbrokers, car salesmen, and telemarketers. As reflected in this poll, you may have heard some stereotypes. Many of them couldn't be further from the truth—so don't let stereotypes steer you away from considering an exciting and prosperous career in sales. You can find out more about the myths of professional selling by accessing the bonuses located at www.10StepsToSales.com/bonuses.

A Brief History of the Sales Profession

The term *profession* comes from the word *profess*. It originally was a religious term referring to an acknowledgment or declaration.

However, a profession is generally defined as an occupation that requires considerable training and specialized study (such as law, medicine, or engineering). The question then becomes, "What is the sales profession?" With less than a handful of undergraduate degrees available that relate to selling, sales professionals are left to their own devices to learn and apply the vast body of knowledge available.

POINTER

I'm not sure where I first heard this, but all salespeople need to understand that your price is never too low—it is just that your customers' perception of the value is too low.
– Terry Metheny, Sales Trainer/Consultant, Terry Metheny and Associates

Early salespeople in America primarily consisted of peddlers or canvassers. Peddlers carried trunks filled with goods; some pulled a wagon or traveled on horseback. They had to go from town to town, build trust, and sell in a very transactional purchase. A canvasser typically represented one product and would develop techniques to best sell that one product to as many people as possible. A canvasser would "canvas" an entire territory, offering the product to everyone they saw or met. An early example of this was the canvassing technique used to sell Ulysses S. Grant's personal memoir by the publishing house that represented him.

Both canvassers and peddlers were part of an ancient tradition that originated in people's basic need to exchange goods and to communicate. As people established economic ties with their neighbors, they traveled extensively all around the world in an effort to trade or barter.

As emigrants began to filter into early American territories in the 18th and 19th centuries, many became salespeople. Like their predecessors, these direct sellers began their treks on trails marked by nature. Good roads developed slowly on the frontiers of early America. Early Native American trails evolved into major roads and eventually turnpikes. As the roadways expanded, the peddler's influence on trade was reinforced.

The first American company to define simple rules of a successful sales process and the corresponding methodologies was the National Cash Register Corporation (NCR) in the late 1800s. The simple philosophy used by NCR was

- know your customer
- know your product
- be ready for the customer to buy
- stay engaged with the customer after the sale.

In the late 1900s, a major shift in selling focus occurred, although still based on the initial processes and techniques of the peddlers and canvassers found in the early 1800s. This shift marks the change from *product-centric* selling to *customer-centric* or *solution* selling. Today, the philosophy of understanding and consulting a customer to develop win–win solutions still exists. Despite these advances, there is still a huge need for sales professionals to build relationships, understand the customer, and bring value to buyers.

Foundations of Professional Selling

The famous football coach Vince Lombardi used to start his football camps by holding a football and stating, "Gentlemen, this is a football." This was his reminder that without basic knowledge, the team could not achieve its goals. The same is true for sales professionals. Before a salesperson can interact effectively with customers, he or she needs to have basic knowledge of the definitions and general sales processes.

POINTER

To be effective and eventually successful, you need to believe in your product, and truly believe that you and your product are helping your prospects. If you don't believe you, they won't either.
– Brent Neitz, Senior Manager, Inside Sales, Sage

A *sale* is a unique transaction with deliverables and an exchange of money or its equivalent. It's important to realize that a sale is not just the transfer of goods or services; rather a sale occurs when

- the full knowledge of a good or service is transferred to the buying organization (or buyer)
- a transaction has taken place
- the product or service meets or exceeds the buying organization's level of expectation or need.

A *transaction* is a distinct event in the overall sales process. When a customer wants the same good or service purchased previously, the most successful sales professionals treat it as a separate transaction.

A *sales process* is a series of tactical and strategic processes that leads to the sales transaction.

How quickly do sales occur? A sales cycle is part of a business process. In most cases, the process starts with some sort of sales cycle that can be as short as a minute (selling a hamburger at a fast-food restaurant) or can last for years (selling an electric generator to a utility company). Effective salespeople understand their sales cycle and its role within their organization's business processes.

Depending on the industry and types of products or services being sold, sales cycles come in different forms and descriptions. They all essentially span the time and process from when the salesperson and the customer decide to do business together through the delivery of the product or service.

These activities usually include researching the customer, phone calls, in-person sales calls, proposals, and pulling all of the right players together to deliver the product or service once the sale is closed.

The essence of selling involves thinking, communicating, and relationship building. Every customer is different, so a salesperson must always be thinking about where he or she is in the selling process and what action to take next.

FIGURE A.1

The Knowledge Transfer Continuum

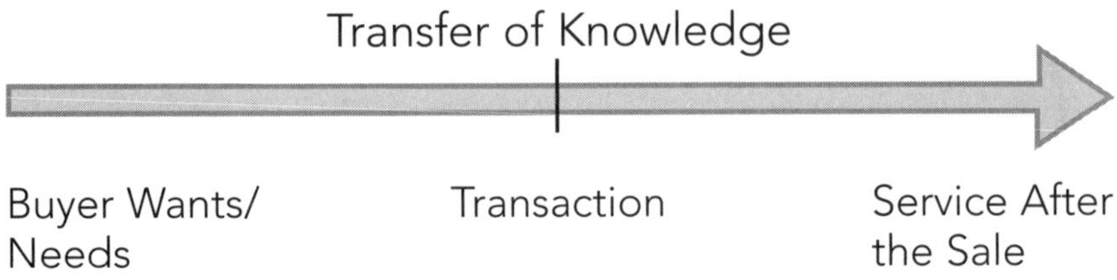

The transaction and knowledge transfer continuum reflects the general steps in a sales cycle.

- During this process, successful salespeople adeptly assess the buyer's current knowledge level, wants, and needs.
- Next, the sales professional skillfully shares knowledge of his or her products or services at a comfortable pace—yet at a pace that attains the revenue goals of the selling organization in a timely manner. Sometimes this transfer of knowledge may take place during phone or face-to-face discussions, via RFP (request for proposal) responses and presentations to an entire group of people, and so on.
- Once this transfer of knowledge occurs, then the sales transaction may take place.

> **POINTER**
> Everyone wants to buy, but no one wants to be sold.
> *– Brian Dunn, Director of Business Development, OPTIMBUY Consulting*

If the sale does occur, the process doesn't stop there—the salesperson should maintain the relationship even during times when other members of the selling organization are responsible for the delivery or implementation of what's been sold.

Learn How to Sell

> "Learning How to Sell" is ***completely*** different than
>
> "Learning Professional Selling"

"Learning how to sell" requires a phone, a desk, a customer, a couple of books on sales, and asking a ton of questions. Eventually, salespeople will figure out how to "do" professional selling. When someone asks how I sell, they are really asking how I carry out a task.

The problem with learning how to sell is that it requires

- hearing "no" frequently until you get it right (which requires persistence)
- failing a lot (which requires a thick skin)
- finding ways to stay constantly motivated (which requires a positive attitude)
- going to a top sales performer and asking them what they did, only to hear things like
    - There are no silver bullets in sales; you just have to do it!
    - You just have to figure it out on your own.
    - If I tell you, it will not help you.
    - It's a numbers game! Just keep making calls, and you'll get it!

"Learning professional selling," in contrast, requires an understanding of theory and practice, as well as why something exists and what it is. It focuses on understanding what selling is rather than how to do it. Learning professional selling requires

- asking what selling is
- learning the systems, theories, and underpinnings of professional selling
- learning how the profession interfaces with other professions

- discovering the systems of professional selling and how they all interact
- learning the sales process
- understanding the aspects of sales decision making
- exploring the legal and ethical limits of the job before being put into a compromising situation
- finding ways to be creative within the sales process.

Understand How Professional Selling Works

Now that you understand the profession of selling lies along the transaction and knowledge transfer continuum, the essence of selling is about closing enough transactions to meet your quota and grow your territory. How do successful sales professionals do it? They identify, qualify, close, and follow up on prospects. Prospects are those individuals or companies who may have a need for your products or services. Targeted prospects are defined as those who are most likely to buy; hence, that's who you should work with to engage in a transaction. To accomplish this, you must engage in a sales process to help you sort out the prospects, targeted prospects, and future customers. Many organizations have their own sales processes that you are required to follow; however, in general you should:

- **Get the attention** of your prospect through some advertising or prospecting method.
- **Hold their interest** by using an appeal that resonates with them. It may be the prestige they will gain, the money they will save in the long run, or their ability to have the latest and most cutting-edge technology.
- **Build their desire** by showing them the benefits of your products or service and painting a convincing picture of what they will attain from using the product or service you are providing.
- **Gain their conviction** by increasing their desire for your product and proving the return they will gain on their investment with your company. Show the worth of your

product or service and compare it to its competitors. Use testimonials from happy customers if you can.

- **Take action.** Encourage the prospect to act. This is your closing. Ask for the order or business. If they object, help them understand better. There are many variations of closing techniques that can help you get the business.

You can revisit the buying and selling process in Steps 6 and 7, but it's important to note that the sales process of today isn't a nice, linear, polished, and simplified series of steps. The sales process is often nonlinear, circular, and continuously evolving. In fact, many would argue it is quite chaotic! The reason is because transactions are continuously evaluated by the buyer. That evaluation continues after the "close" of the transaction and the check is written. Many times, sales professionals can sell upgrades (up-sell) or other products (cross-sell) to their clients based on the success of the post-transaction experience. This means it's hard to tell when and where the sales process starts and ends.

Define What Sales Success Means for You

All sales professionals enter the profession for their own reasons. Many salespeople land in the profession after testing nearly every other profession first. Others determine that selling is right for them early in working years or while still in college.

Regardless of the path taken to enter the sales profession, all great salespeople define success in their own way. The key to this success is to decide what the most important element of success is for you. Be careful when defining what "success" is for yourself; this is a very personal decision.

Because professional selling is the growth engine in an organization, your definition of sales success should include capturing enough revenue in your sales territory to exceed the quota set by management. This is important not only because it will keep you employed, but it's also the only definition that matters to the business world. Individuals who repeatedly meet or exceed their quotas are thought of as "successful."

To get you started in defining the elements of what sales success means to you, some examples may be helpful:

- acquisition of power
- acquisition of money
- impact to the organization or to the community (feeling of being "significant")
- helping others
- providing for family needs.

Understand That Your Attitude and Mindset Matter

Now that you've defined what sales success means to you, the biggest contributor to your success will be your own attitude and positive mental image. After that, the types of products or services you sell (and the perceived value of those products and services by buyers in the market), the internal support you receive (in getting answers to questions, supporting clients, or fixing problems), and the availability of resources (such as time, information, and technology) are key contributors to your ability to succeed. Just remember, great salespeople never let factors outside their direct control hinder achieving success for too long.

Keep in mind that there is no such thing as a "perfect" product or service; nor is there a "flawless sale." There are always concerns, problems, and issues to address in every sales situation. However, the most successful sales professionals don't get discouraged; they expect these situations and overcome them. More important, they learn from them. Ultimately, sales success boils down to ensuring that the relationships and conversations created with the customer are successful and mutually beneficial despite any hiccups in the company or sales situation.

Not long ago, when the market was less competitive, many sales professionals would sell a product or service, get the ink on the contract, and move on with little or no regard for maintaining the relationship after the sale. Without actively maintaining relationships built during the sales process, these same salespeople would receive calls from unhappy customers to discuss a flawed implementation or a piece of machinery that didn't work—or they would simply express their desire to move on to another partner or vendor.

Remember the "golden rule" in selling: treat others as you want to be treated. Put yourself into their shoes. Stay positive.

Find What Works for You

The sales profession is a complex system of human emotion, global economics, and sales competence. Go to any bookstore and look at the sales section to see the entire breadth of knowledge needed to succeed. As a result, the most successful salespeople enter the profession and become lifelong learners actively continuing personal education and training.

How do you become a student of selling? Reading every book is not the answer. Book knowledge typically focuses on different aspects of an overall sales process. You can spend months or years reading about the different approaches to building relationships, communicating, approaching sales territories, managing the process, becoming a better leader, managing time, leveraging technology, customer service, and so on. Unfortunately there is no magical *one* right way to sell.

> **POINTER**
> To be successful is very simple. Be persistent and do what you say you will do.
> – *Kevin Shaughness, Field Sales, Electro Enterprises*

Many successful sales professionals will tell you that what works for them might not work for you. Sales professionals rarely fully revamp their entire sales process based on learning any one new approach; rather, they customize what they have learned over their years of selling into their own unique and personalized way of doing things. This customized approach, as refined throughout the span of professional careers, becomes a unique sales methodology or system. While you may hear that the sales process or sales funnel is extremely important, you'll discover that creativity and flexibility within that sales process requires your own unique approach. Think of the sales process as a guide and make it work for you!

To help you though the process of lifelong learning and finding what works for you, a Recommended Reading list is available in Appendix C on page 233.

Determine Where You're Going

The speed of business and the choices that buyers have create unique demands on salespeople. It's not how big the organization is, it's the ability of the sales professionals to be nimble and quickly change their environment that makes the difference. Why? Because customers have become more cost conscious and demanding. They are better educated, more discriminating, and more informed than ever before.

Moreover, the rapid expansion of buyer choices dictates the need for a competent salesperson to help determine the best choice for solving a particular issue. Products and services are growing at an alarming rate—for example, it is estimated that there are more than 1 million different types of consumer products available on the market today. It is further estimated that the average family only buys from about 150 of them!

These change factors have caused company executives to seek the answer to one important question—who can make the cut? You can, if

- you show how you can help outdistance the current and future competitors

- you are creative in the way you market and sell your products
- you clearly "differentiate" your company from the competition
- you are willing to help take calculated risks to introduce new features and innovative products to the marketplace that your customers are demanding
- you focus on the voice of the customer
- you continuously improve, every day, every minute
- you develop customer relationships and establish a reputation for outstanding customer service
- you have the ability to learn faster than your competitors
- you understand and utilize technology in the right way.

In summary, sales professionals play one of the most mission-critical roles in an organization—driving revenue. Selling in today's world is extremely complex. Salespeople are the "face" of an organization and carry the tremendous responsibility of identifying opportunities, building trust, developing creative solutions, mitigating client land mines, and ensuring that prospects evolve into satisfied, loyal customers.

The most successful sales professionals recognize the importance of not only understanding their role in relation to the buyer but also optimizing their personal strengths.

WORKSHEET A.1

Charting the Course to My Own Success

What does success in selling look like to you? Many people think that salespeople are only driven by money. While money may be a factor in your decision to be a great salesperson, it's rarely the only reason to work hard, learn quickly, and overcome challenges.

Success means different things to different people. To develop a powerful success strategy, you must first have a clear concept of what success means to you.

So, what's in it for you? What elements of sales success do you require to receive the most out of the sales profession?

My elements of sales success are driven by my perceptions about what?

Money is . . .

Wealth is . . .

Rich people are . . .

Successful people are . . .

What success means to me:

My personal mission statement is: (*Tip!* Take the example above and reword it if you need help getting started!)

My personal mission is to . . .

The reasons I can't or may not have success include:

Some of the possible negatives about being extremely successful or going through the process of trying to become extremely successful are...

My greatest worries, fears, and concerns regarding success and wealth are . . .

---

continued on next page

Worksheet A.1, continued

The worst thing about success is . . .

The best thing about success is . . .

How would your life change if you became extremely successful? What would you have to lose? What would you gain?

What kind of person would you become if you achieved great success?

A P P E N D I X B

Top Ten Myths of Selling

You have probably heard a lot of different opinions about the sales profession. Let's face it—some of what you heard might not be the most positive. You know what? That's fine, because here's the truth. The sales profession is one of the most sought-after professions in the world. Not only that, it is one in which you can work hard and achieve the highest compensation of your life, and it's a profession where you are the driver and fulfiller of your own destiny. Each day is a new opportunity to build new relationships; find new ways to make an impact; continue to build respect, trust, and credibility with existing clients; and provide a much-needed revenue source for your company. However, there are some myths that must be dispelled to provide a better sense of what the profession and sales professionals are all about.

Myth 1: All Salespeople Are Shady!

In the Broadway play *Death of a Salesman*, Willy Loman was a down-and-out, emotionally spent salesman trying to understand his life after 34 years of traveling up and down the roads selling his products. The negative stereotype of a salesman is deeply rooted in the subconscious of society.

POINTER

It's all about the customer and his or her needs. The more you can determine what their needs and wants are, and find solutions to them, the more successful you will be.
– Adolph P. Kaestner, Professional Speaker and Trainer

In all fairness, almost everyone has had a "bad" buying experience—which tends to conjure up images of the fast-talking, scheming, shady, over-the-top, and high-pressure salesperson. As a result, clients feel burned and incorrectly jump to the conclusion that all salespeople are shady. Ironically, *all* professions (not just selling) can have fast-talking, scheming, shady, over-the-top, and high-pressure people in them. Likewise, all professions have extremely professional individuals.

Some examples of behavior that reinforces this negative stereotype include

- salespeople who simply pitch their product and do not converse with the client to understand their needs and propose the most appropriate products or solutions
- salespeople who do not prepare for or practice the delivery of a presentation before a sales call
- salespeople who share all the product factoids but do not explain "what's in it for the buyer" and how their solution can benefit the client, solve a problem, and deliver the value promised
- salespeople who don't listen, and at the end of the sale they ask for the order without building trust
- salespeople who don't treat their job as a profession, but look for the shortcut or the easiest way to close a sale, without regard for the needs, values, or requests of the customer
- salespeople who don't make the right decision, no matter how "inconvenient" that decision might be for them or their management.

In fact, the highest performing sales professionals do exactly the opposite of the behaviors just listed.

Myth 2: If You're a Schmoozer, Then You're a Closer!

A schmoozer is someone who has the ability to converse casually, especially to gain an advantage or make a social connection. This is almost the definition of *networking* in business terms. Closers, on the other hand, are successful sales professionals who get the client to say "yes" and secure the sale.

Make no mistake; schmoozers are not closers because they are only interested in one thing when talking with a client—manipulating the conversation in an attempt to make money. The most successful sales professionals are authentic and genuine when building trust, rapport, and relationships. Building "fake rapport" is something that people can smell for miles away, so don't do it. Schmoozing doesn't help you close deals—successful networking does.

The most successful sales professionals work hard to first develop a personal connection with prospects and clients, and then they develop a plan to truly help the prospect or client who will reap the rewards. In other words, if you give, you will receive! Schmoozing doesn't allow for that—it is all about getting, with no giving.

Myth 3: Sales Ethics Don't Exist!

Every day people are faced with ethical challenges in business. Ethical decisions mean making the right decision even when nobody is looking and realizing that an ultimate payback may take time to attain.

A company's ethics and integrity are directly reflected in the relationship between a salesperson and the customer. As a result, most great sales professionals who have been selling for any length of time have had to build their "sales reputation" through satisfied clients. You cannot be unethical in the sales profession and stay at the top of your game and build a client base that considers you to be a trusted advisor.

POINTER

Hug your customer! Give him or her all your honest attention! And be really interested in his or her business.
– *Esther Buitenhuis, Sales Manager*

As an example, you will come to realize that your decision to work with the client affects the profit and loss issues of your company as well as theirs. Business relationships affect how much business you are able to conduct in the future and the quality of the relationships you build with your customers. The best decisions are those that consider both the short-term and long-term effects and that keep the client's success at the forefront. More important, the decisions you make can solidify your standing and reputation as someone to look to for answers, advice, and recommendations.

Myth 4: Marketing and Selling Are the Same Thing!

A professor I had once said, "In business you can do three things: make it, sell it, or count it." With respect to "selling it," the definition comprises two divergent but inextricably entwined functions—sales and marketing. Perhaps in today's world, a more appropriate description is that you can only make it, *grow* it, or count it.

Why reference growth rather than selling? Ultimately each function needs the other if the company is to grow. To that end, sales and marketing are separate but equal professions from a business perspective.

How should both sales and marketing professionals work together? Many marketers believe that marketing should play the dominant role. After all, marketing defines the product, articulates the positioning, and creates all the sales tools (ranging from glowing CEO profiles in *Fortune* magazine to the corporate logo). All sales has to do is to follow orders, right?

Salespeople believe that selling should play the dominant role. After all, selling is where the rubber meets the road, where the tough get going, where everyone gives 110 percent, and where slogans reign supreme. Salespeople bring home the bacon.

Both functions are required. But selling and marketing are not the same thing. Both departments should agree on the need to stay focused on what clients want in an effort to provide value.

Myth 5: Selling Is About Winning Over Your Customer!

Selling isn't about winning over anyone. It's about helping a customer win over their problems. Thinking of making a sale as "winning" means someone has to lose. If you are winning and your customers are losing, you'll be selling a very, very short amount of time. It's about *both* the customer and you winning.

Myth 6: Professional Selling Isn't a Real Profession!

If you're embarrassed about being in the sales profession, this is the myth you're subscribing to. You have to be proud of being in sales to be successful. One way to do this is to realize that you can help the people you'll be working with on a daily basis to capitalize on business opportunities or to solve business challenges. Salespeople regularly engage with business professionals from a variety of formalized professions, including

- Chief financial officer (formalized by the American Finance Association)
- Legal counsel (formalized by the American Bar Association)
- Project manager (formalized by the Project Management Institute)
- Marketing professional (formalized by the American Marketing Association)
- Information technology professional (formalized by numerous associations and organizations)

- Procurement professional (formalized by the Institute of Supply Management and the National Association of Purchasing Management).

There are five attributes generally identified as common to all recognized professions (Meginson, Mosley, & Pietrie 1986). Think about each in relation to the sales profession:

- **A Unique Body of Knowledge**—This attribute encompasses concepts and principles that are unique to the profession and are documented so that they can be studied and learned through formal education. In most professions, the body of knowledge is taught in graduate or professional schools. For example, the specialized body of knowledge of the legal profession is taught in law schools. A degree does not necessarily qualify an individual to practice in the profession, but it does provide a means of ensuring that the individual has at least been exposed to the basic principles on which the profession is based. Every profession has at least one degree that can be earned by those wishing to demonstrate knowledge of the profession's principles.
- **Standards of Entry**—Defined minimum standards of entry into a profession imply progression in a career. Entry standards define the place from where a career path begins. All professionals must have an accepted route open to the public by which a person can become a recognized member of the profession. Law, engineering, accounting, medicine, and teaching all have entry standards. These standards usually involve formal education leading to an academic degree, several years of experience in an apprenticeship program or as a beginner in the profession, test score requirements, which may or may not be legally enforceable, or some combination of the three.
- **A Code of Ethics**—Ethical standards, or a code of ethics, is common to most professions. Its purpose is to make explicit appropriate behavior and to provide a basis for self-policing of unethical behavior, thus avoiding or limiting the necessary legal controls.

- **Service Orientation to the Profession**—The service orientation is an attribute by which members are committed to bettering the profession itself. Professionals commit their money and energy to publishing their ideas and experience, attending conventions, and generally contributing to the body of knowledge and the administration of the profession. In some cases, commitment to the profession is stronger than to the employer—as seen in cases where professionals leave a job rather than violate the profession's standards or ethical practice.
- **A Sanctioning Organization**—The authenticating body or sanctioning organization has many purposes. It sets the standard and acts as a self-policing agency. It promotes publications and exchange of ideas, encourages research, develops and administers certification programs, and sponsors and accredits education programs. Through public information and recognition of professionals, such organizations provide the voice for their profession. To summarize, the purpose of the authenticating body is to administer the profession.

> Salespeople have rights too! Nonprofit trade associations dedicated to the profession try to help organizations realize the value of their salespeople. More important, these organizations have attempted to branch out and support the attributes previously listed.
>
> To find out more about these types of organizations, contact
>
> - National Association of Sales Professionals: www.nasp.com
> - Strategic Account Management Association: www.strategicaccounts.org
> - Sales Training Drivers: www.SalesTrainingDrivers.org
> - Sales and Marketing Executives International: www.smei.org

Myth 7: Anyone Can Sell!

Selling is a hard profession to master. It's one of the most complicated professions in the world. Where else do you have to understand organizations and individuals with such depth and clarity?

Where else do you have to build rapport with so many different types of people, in so many different locations, buildings, or business types?

On top of this complexity is the reality that selling is one of the few real pay-for-performance professions, with more than half of the compensation at risk or based on a variable commission. A lot of sales professionals feel stress in their jobs. In the engineering profession, stress results from the application of a constant force to an immovable object. In selling, the force is your quota and the immovable object is your customer's expectations. But take heart—with hard work, tips, and a sound sales process, you can reap vast rewards from all of your effort.

Myth 8: Selling Is a Numbers Game!

"Selling is a numbers game" is a phrase you will probably hear early in your career. Make the calls, make the presentations, and work your way through enough people, and eventually you will make a sale. The theory goes something like this: the more phone calls you make, the more sales you will close. For example, make 100 phone calls. Of those 100, send 10 proposals. And of those 10, you will close two.

This approach is shortsighted, and this myth can lead to a dangerous philosophy—a philosophy that dictates no matter what, you always have to do more. Before subscribing to this philosophy, remember—*quality* always supersedes *quantity*. The most successful sales professionals find a way to stay ahead of the competition and get results *no matter what the numbers say*. It is better to make two phone calls and close two sales than make 100 calls and close two. The key is to be calling on the right people, who have a *want* and a *need*.

For example, an insurance organization provides its sales representatives with contact lists to sell their life insurance and investment products. The problem is most of the prospects on the list live in a low-income area and are highly unlikely to buy life insurance because they don't need or want it. In this case, the numbers game doesn't matter as much—and the representatives are wasting their time.

POINTER

The ideal is not merely telling the truth. It is finding the truth and living the truth. Keep your word, accomplish your promises, over deliver and under commit.
– Tony Ponceti, Sales Manager, Solutions by Magnolia

Rather than buying into the myth that selling is a numbers game, think of a game of darts. By aiming your effort (the dart) at a clearly defined target (your pre-qualified prospect on the dart board), your chances for hitting the mark (a sale) are greatly enhanced. Quality over quantity. Set goals and manage what you forecast. That's the new sales math.

Myth 9: You Must Like Rejection!

Many sales courses, books, and sales training tell you to keep a stiff upper lip when faced with rejection. A rejection can occur when you are rebuffed on the phone, not granted an appointment, or simply told no. These courses will also tell you not to let a "no" get you down. The problem with this approach is the fact that once you accept the simple proposition that you have been rejected in the first place, you have given up the psychological high ground and put your self-esteem into retreat. Simply put, your sales team needs to reject the notion of rejection.

Salespeople are in a profession geared to helping people. If prospects don't want help or choose not to do business with a company for whatever reason, it is not the salesperson's problem. The goal should be to locate another prospect that needs the company's products or services.

In general, the healthiest mindset a sales professional can embody with regard to rejection is: "You, Mr./Ms. Prospect, have made a decision to move forward without our services. I'll be here when you come to your senses and change your mind. It's not our responsibility to straighten you or your company out."

Get used to hearing no, but don't consider it to be rejection—it's just an opportunity to improve!

Myth 10: Selling Is a Dead-End Job!

Do you know that many of the company leaders and entrepreneurs in business today were once salespeople? They carried sample cases, made cold calls, dialed for dollars, did product demonstrations, and handled objections. Today, they're the majority of corporate presidents, CEOs, and the like. Selling is a dead-end job all right—especially when you consider that the end of the job may lead to the seat at the very top of an organization!

This appendix focused on demystifying the top 10 myths of selling. The key take away for you is, "If you guess, you stress." It's that simple. Selling is about taking the guesswork out of what the future will hold. The key is to learn the truth about the sales profession and banish the myths. When you accomplish this, you will find selling concepts that make sense can immediately put into practice. Above all else, the most successful sales professionals persevere when others quit. Perseverance makes a difference to a company's bottom line and whether a sales professional succeeds or not.

Many stereotypes taint the sales profession. Sales professionals are the rainmakers—revenue producers that companies in all industries are looking for to generate revenue for their organizations.

WORKSHEET B.1

Demystifying the Myths—What Is Your Belief?

Instructions: Take a moment to think about the pros and cons of selling based on your beliefs. Complete the sections of this worksheet by indicating the positives (pros) and negatives (cons) of selling with as much detail as possible.

Tip! Keep this worksheet handy and revisit your beliefs as you work through the 10 Steps in this book.

Category	Your Thoughts
Pros of Selling	Examples: ◆ They get to see many different people and many different organizations. ◆ Pay is based on performance. You work harder, you get paid more. Your thoughts? ◆ ◆ ◆ ◆ ◆
Cons of Selling	Examples: ◆ People have negative stereotypes. ◆ Easy to get "caught up" in the performance of the job. Your thoughts? ◆ ◆ ◆ ◆ ◆

continued on next page

Worksheet B.1, continued

Category	Your Thoughts
What Do Professional Salespeople Do Well? (Specifically, what do they do?)	*Tip!* Don't worry if you cannot fill it all in now . . . you'll be able to fill it in more as you read this book. Examples: ◆ Listen before speaking ◆ Become an expert about industries and products ◆ Build lasting relationships Your thoughts? ◆ ◆ ◆ ◆ ◆
What Are Some Behaviors to Avoid (Cons) in Selling? (Specifically, what not to do!)	*Tip!* Don't worry if you cannot fill it all in now . . . you'll be able to fill it in more as you read this book. Examples: ◆ Taking buyers for granted ◆ Being aggressive, pushy, or forceful in conversations ◆ Creating a win–lose scenario with buyers Your thoughts? ◆ ◆ ◆ ◆ ◆

APPENDIX C

Recommended Reading

The 7 Habits of Highly Effective People

by Stephen R. Covey

A groundbreaker when it was first published in 1990, this book continues to be a business bestseller with more than 10 million copies sold. Stephen Covey, an internationally respected leadership authority, realizes that true success encompasses a balance of personal and professional effectiveness, so this book is a manual for performing better in both arenas. His anecdotes are as frequently from family situations as from business challenges.

10 Secrets of Time Management for Salespeople: Gain the Competitive Edge and Make Every Second Count

by Dave Kahle

The typical salesperson today is overwhelmed, and trapped in a chaotic, pressure-filled environment with too much to do and not enough time to do it. Salespeople need help! This book provides it. Dave Kahle contends that smart time management is not about cramming more activity into each hour, but about achieving greater results in that hour. The content has been honed in hundreds of seminars and refined by the perceptions and experiences of thousands of salespeople. *10 Secrets of Time Management for Salespeople* provides powerful, practical insights and ideas that really work, including hundreds of specific, practical, effective time management tips from dozens of salespeople who are on the "front lines" every day.

The 12 Clichés of Selling (and Why They Work)

by Barry J. Farber

This is a good book on why the old tried-and-true things you heard from the "seasoned sales pro" might just work after all.

Buyer-Approved Selling: Sales Strategies from the Buyer's Side of the Desk

by Michael Schell

Schell interviews 228 professional buyers and focuses almost entirely on the sales process from the buyer's perspective. Great read no matter how long you have been in sales or who you call on.

Consultative Selling: The Hanan Formula for High-Margin Sales at High Levels

by Mack Hanan

This is a classic must-have and in every top producer's library! The focus is on how to become a consultant to the executives of your targeted companies. This isn't lip service—he really shows you how to do it!

Cracking the Networking CODE: Four Steps to Priceless Business Relationships

by Dean Lindsay

Networking is one area that you have to do well in. This book addresses how to get comfortable meeting new people and building on the meetings. The CODE in this book breaks down the steps to successful networking and makes it much less intimidating.

Discover Your Sales Strengths: How the World's Greatest Salespeople Develop Winning Careers

by Benson Smith and Tony Rutigliano

Unlike many how-to-sell books written by motivational gurus and successful salespeople, Smith and Rutigliano's work is backed up by facts and figures gleaned from 40 years of Gallup research. The authors, both Gallup consultants, dissect stereotypes and debunk popular "myths" about selling to determine that there is no one formula for success, and that training, knowledge, and experience cannot make a great salesperson. Instead, they find, great salesmanship stems from exploiting individual talents. Top salespeople succeed by figuring out what they do best and then finding a way and a place to do it.

Getting to Yes: Negotiating Agreement Without Giving In

by Roger Fisher and William L. Ury

We're constantly negotiating in our lives, whether it's convincing the kids to do their homework or settling million-dollar lawsuits. For those who need help winning these battles, Roger Fisher has developed a simple and straightforward five-step system for how to behave in negotiations.

Goals: How to Get Everything You Want—Faster Than You Ever Thought Possible

by Brian Tracy

Though goal setting is often over-intellectualized, achievement expert Brian Tracy makes the process come to life as an essential ingredient for any type of personal development. He's been refining these ideas for 20 years, and no important insight is overlooked. Tracy's extraordinary thinking is always expressed in practical action steps.

Hired Gun: You're #1, and Somebody Hates It

by Robert Workman

While every salesperson should read *Hired Gun*, it is not a book on how to sell, but rather a guide to discovering your personal identity and learning why it is your most precious asset in sales. Trust Workman—if you're a top gun, you can bet there is someone gunning for you. This book tells you why. You'll learn why top sales producers scare the hell out of those who manage them. Workman's sales personality evaluation test alone is worth the price of the book. *Hired Gun* is iconoclastic, quirky, rambling, and very funny—perfect. It is exactly the book you would expect from a cigar-smoking, Ferrari-driving Texan who lives in a converted warehouse with his pet cougar.

How to Connect in Business in 90 Seconds or Less

by Nicholas Boothman

This book is not about a new business theory; it's about how you can become more successful in business by learning to connect with your customers, colleagues, bosses, employees, and even total strangers in 90 seconds or less. Armed with simple tools that include eye contact, attitude, body movements, and voice techniques, the average person can become a more successful communicator. Boothman is a vibrant writer with a fine wit that maintains the reader's attention by way of effective person-to-person scenarios that correspond to average daily encounters. Whether employed in sales, education, business, or even public speaking, effective communication is mandatory, and Boothman's techniques may be the express ticket necessary to progress to that next level.

How to Master the Art of Selling

by Tom Hopkins

This book launched more than 3 million real estate and selling careers worldwide. It's considered the world's best reference guide for selling and has been used for more than 17 years in every sales profession. Even if you've been selling for years, you'll find page after page of valuable information guaranteed to help you serve more clients while boosting your bank account.

How to Win Friends and Influence People

by Dale Carnegie

This is the bible of building relationships and a classic book on getting along with virtually anyone. In sales, relationships are everything, and if you have not read this book, go buy it now!

Integrity Selling for the 21st Century: How to Sell How People Buy

by Ron Willingham

If you've tried manipulative, self-focused selling techniques that demean you and your customer, or if you've ever wondered if selling could be more than just talking people into buying, then *Integrity Selling for the 21st Century* is the book for you. Its concept is simple: Only by getting to know your customers and their needs—and believing that you can meet those needs—will you enjoy relationships with customers built on trust. And only then, when you bring more value to your customers than you receive in payment, will you begin to reap the rewards of high sales.

Let's Get Real, or Let's Not Play: Transforming the Buyer/Seller Relationship

by Mahan Khalsa

This book teaches you to become totally client-focused, break down the barriers of dysfunctional business development, and find rewarding, productive business relationships. With honesty, clarity, and authenticity, the book cuts through the nonsense and focuses on getting results and helping clients succeed.

Maximum Achievement: Strategies and Skills That Will Unlock Your Hidden Powers to Succeed

by Brian Tracy

Brian Tracy has been one of my success mentors for years. His wisdom is clear and eloquent—but more than that, it is right on! Even before you finish reading *Maximum Achievement* for the first time, you will be a changed person—it's that incredible. I say first time because you will want to read it again and again.

Tracy covers all of the proactive bases: smart thinking, system thinking, futuristic thinking, and positive thinking. If you are truly seeking the kind of success and abundance that makes your life 100 percent livable, you must read this book. Many of his ideas are found in *Success Bound: Breaking Free of Mediocrity* by Randy Gilbert, another book built on learning how to be responsible and live proactively.

Everything I have put into practice that he has recommended has worked. The laws of success in this book will bring you success. Read it and you will believe that you can do anything you set your mind to. My copy is well worn with highlighter and pen marks all through it from the numerous times that I've returned to it in order to study it again.

The New Strategic Selling: The Unique Sales System Proven Successful by the World's Best Companies, Revised and Updated for the 21st Century

by Stephen E. Heiman and Diane Sanchez

This is a great book from a strategic selling perspective (not tactical). If you are involved in complex sales with multiple decision makers and influencers, get this book. It will help you navigate your way through the organization.

Positioning: The Battle for Your Mind

by Al Ries and Jack Trout

This is the definitive book on positioning, a concept developed by the authors. It talks about how to deal with the problems of communicating in an overcommunicated society. Witty and fast-paced, this book spells out how to position a market leader so that it gets into the mind and stays there, position a follower in a way that finds a "hole" not occupied by the leader, and avoid the pitfalls of letting a second product ride on the coattails of an established one. Revised to reflect significant developments in the five years since its original publication, *Positioning* reveals the fascinating case histories and anecdotes behind the campaigns of many stunning successes and failures in the world of advertising.

The Sales Bible: The Ultimate Sales Resource, Revised Edition

by Jeffrey Gitomer

Gitomer provides motivational advice and practical techniques for initiating, maintaining, and closing a sales presentation. Written in a breezy manner with short, easy-to-remember suggestions, this book should prove popular with persons just getting started in this field or those needing an inspirational pep talk. In an area where there are literally dozens of works already available, this isn't an essential purchase, but it will prove helpful to anyone who reads it. It is usually accompanied by flash cards and a computer disk on sales techniques.

Selling 101: What Every Successful Sales Professional Needs to Know

by Zig Ziglar

Short, compact, and concise, this book focuses on the basics of how to persuade more people more effectively, more ethically, and more often. Ziglar draws from his fundamental selling experiences and shows that while the basics of selling may remain constant, salespeople must continue learning, living, and looking—learning from the past without living there; living in the present by seizing each vital moment of every single day; and looking to the future with hope, optimism, and education. His tips will not only keep your clients happy and add to your income, but will also teach you ideas and principles that will, most importantly, add to the quality of your life.

Selling to Big Companies

by Jill Konrath

Friendly, fresh, filled with insights, and guaranteed to rev up the performance of anyone selling in the business-to-business marketplace. Penetrating large accounts has never been tougher. The challenge of finding decision makers' names and breaking through voicemail is huge.

Selling to VITO (The Very Important Top Officer)

by Anthony Parinello

Full of ideas on how to reach executives, this book works if you are willing to do what it says. You will need to do some experimenting, observing, and fine-tuning, but Parinello's ideas will pay off in the end.

Solution Selling: Creating Buyers in Difficult Selling Markets

by Michael Bosworth

This book is a resource for sales managers in large account or corporate sales, with specific advice on assigning leads, managing the sales process, and controlling costs. Effective techniques for prospecting, overcoming objections, and creating value are also covered.

SPIN Selling

by Neil Rackham

This is the definitive work on how to ask questions. What makes it different is the amount of research it is based upon. This is a very popular system and it works.

Think and Grow Rich

by Napoleon Hill

Napolean Hill was a very successful individual. When Hill met with Andrew Carnegie, he was offered only a place to stay and no salary. Here was Hill with pennies in his pockets, sitting in front of the richest man in the world at that time, who offered Hill no financial remuneration. Carnegie felt that if Hill were to write a book about how to create wealth, then Hill would have to become wealthy himself—and he did. *Think and Grow Rich* is a classic that should be read by everyone. Over the last 30 years or so, I have encountered many successful people from various walks of life who attribute *Think and Grow Rich* with helping them reach new limits in success.

Ultimate Selling Power: How to Create and Enjoy a Multimillion Dollar Sales Career

by Donald J. Moine and Ken Lloyd

Ultimate Selling Power reveals how average salespeople in a variety of industries have created multimillion-dollar careers using many powerful, newly developed sales and marketing techniques. It is a practical, step-by-step guide showing what the best, most successful salespeople in the world are doing to attract an almost unlimited number of customers and clients and to close a record-breaking number of sales.

You Can't Teach a Kid to Ride a Bike at a Seminar: The Sandler Sales Institute's 7-Step System for Successful Selling

by David H. Sandler

One of the most thought-provoking books on selling that I have read, this is a "straight-to-the-point" type of sales methodology. It is great for putting you in the proper mindset and really thinking about things from your position. Sandler was one of the first to recommend "qualify or disqualify and then move on!" Most sales books focus only on a sales process or skills. Sandler focuses on both, plus attitude and behavior often ignored by others.

APPENDIX D

Sales Terms You Should Know

> **Sales lingo is a "competency thermometer" for how well you understand what selling is.** Some of the most commonly used sales terms are found on the following pages.

Account Management. A tactical and strategic planning process that assists a salesperson in meeting specific selling objectives before, during, and after a solution is sold. It is specific to one account (meaning it is already a customer). The outcome of the account management process is a "balanced portfolio" of accounts with a strategy and corresponding tactics for increasing revenue from each relationship.

Benefit. A benefit is a solution attribute expressed in terms of what the buyer receives from the solution rather than its physical characteristics or features. Benefits are often paired with specific features, but they need not be. They are perceived, not necessarily real. One benefit of driving is freedom; another is cost-effective transportation.

Business-to-Business (B2B). An organization that is focused on business-to-business transactions. A business engaged in selling to another business.

Buyer. A buyer is someone who accepts the seller's quotation for the sale of the solution or whose order for the solution is accepted by the seller. A buying organization is any company, association, team, person, or governmental body that has been identified as needing to purchase a product and/or service. A buying organization can be a suspect, prospect, or current/previous customer or client to the selling organization.

Client. A customer who is regularly and actively engaged by the selling organization.

Closing (aka deal close). Closing is a sales term that refers to the process of making a sale. Specifically, it refers to reaching the final step, which may be an exchange of money or acquiring a signature.

Salespeople are often taught to think of targets not as strangers, but rather as prospective customers who already want or need what is being sold. Such prospects need only be "closed." The term is usually distinguished from ordinary practices such as explaining a product's benefits or justifying an expense. "Closing" is usually reserved for more artful means of persuasion. For example, a salesman might mention that his product is popular with a person's neighbors, knowing that people tend to follow perceived trends.

Commission. A fee or percentage of a sale allowed to a sales representative or an agent for services rendered.

Compensation Plan (aka comp plan). Compensation plans consist of a series of decisions that form a framework for rewarding employees for their participation and productivity, which result in the successful performance of the organization. Since each person is different, these decisions must be able to be applied in varying circumstances while retaining the consistency required for equity. In this way, the employment exchange is an individual exchange between the person and the organization based on the variations in perception of each. In some cases, groups of employees have similar circumstances and/or perceptions that have led organizations to develop compensation programs that contain enough special characteristics to be dealt with separately.

Consultative Selling. Consultative selling involves deeper questioning of the prospect about organizational and operational issues that can typically extend beyond a specific product or solution in and of itself. This leads to greater understanding of the prospect's wider needs (particularly those affected by the product), and the questioning process itself also results in greater trust, rapport, and empathy between salesperson and buyer. The process has been practiced instinctively in good salespeople and organizations for many years, particularly since the 1970s, especially for concept selling or service solutions selling, driven by competitive pressures, as buyers began to learn as much about the sales process and techniques as the salespeople themselves. In the 1970s and 1980s, various proprietary frameworks and models were established, and many of these remain in use today.

Cost of Goods Sold. The cost of goods sold describes the direct expenses incurred in producing a particular product or service (solution) for sale, including the actual cost of materials that comprise the solution, and direct labor expense in putting the solution in working condition. Cost of goods sold does not include indirect expenses such as office expenses, accounting, shipping, advertising, and other expenses that cannot be attributed to a particular item for sale. Subtracting the cost of goods sold from the amount billed when selling the solution (sales revenue) produces the gross profit on the good.

Cross-Sell. The sale of a product or service in addition to the product or service the customer has already purchased, but from a different product line. For example, an agent may sell an additional service such as broadband Internet with a new telephone service. You can only cross-sell to existing customers. This is almost the same as up-sell, it's just delineating the fact that the additional sale to an existing customer was for a *different line of product*, not the same as originally purchased.

Customer. A buying organization that (may) buy repeatedly but is not regularly or actively engaged by the selling organization. *See also*, client.

Feature. Features are the way benefits are provided to consumers. The tire feature of a car allows the car to roll down the road. Usually any one of several different features may be chosen to meet a customer need. For example, a car with a steering wheel *and* tires will not only allow the car to roll down the road, it will also allow the person to keep it on the road.

Gross Margin. Gross margin is an ambiguous phrase that expresses the relationship between gross profit and sales revenue. The ambiguity arises because it can be expressed in absolute terms:

$$\text{Gross Margin} = \text{Revenue} - \text{Cost of Goods Sold}$$

Or as the ratio of gross profit to sales revenue, usually in the form of a percentage:

$$\text{Gross Margin Percentage} = 100 \times (\text{Revenue} - \text{Cost of Goods Sold})$$

In everyday speech, the word *percentage* is sometimes omitted and this can create confusion. Higher gross margins for a manufacturer reflect greater efficiency in turning raw materials into income. For a retailer, it will be their markup over wholesale. Larger gross margins are generally good for companies, with the exception of discount retailers. They need to show that operations efficiency and financing allows them to operate with tiny margins.

Need Identification. In this stage, the salesperson takes a qualified prospect through a series of question-and-answer sessions in order to identify the requirements of the prospect. During this step, the salesperson will attempt to help the buyer identify and quantify a business need or a "gap" between where the client is today and where they would like to be in the future. Based on that gap, needs can be clarified to determine if the solution will fill all, or part of, the overall gap. From this procedure the salesperson is able to come up with a proposal suggesting various products or services that will meet the need as presented by the prospect.

Pricing. Price is the amount of currency to be paid. Pricing is a strategy as determined by one of the four Ps of marketing. The other three parts of the marketing mix are product, promotion, and placement. Pricing is the manual or automatic process of applying prices to purchase and sales orders based on factors such as a fixed amount, quantity break, promotion or sales campaign, specific vendor quote, price prevailing on entry, shipment or invoice date, combination of multiple orders or lines, and many others. Automated systems require more setup and maintenance but may prevent pricing errors.

Profit Margin. Profit margin is a measure of profitability. It is calculated as

Net Income / Revenue = Profit Margin (expressed as a percentage)

For example, suppose a company produces bread and sells it for $5. It costs the company $3 to produce the bread and it also had to pay an additional $1 in tax. That makes the company's net income $1 (5 – (3 + 1)) and its revenue $5. The profit margin would be (1 / 5) or 20 percent. Profit margin is an indicator of a company's pricing policies and its ability to control costs. Differences in competitive strategy and product mix cause profit margins to vary among different companies.

Proposal. A business proposal is a requirement in complex sales. Clients sometimes issue a Request for Proposal (RFP) from which a proposal must be written, or, after needs identification, the salesperson creates a proposal that attempts to fill the needs as expressed by the buyer.

A properly accomplished proposal will educate the prospective client about the full nature of his or her need. Often, a prospective client may be aware of only a portion of the need they expressed during needs identification. Hopefully, the proposal persuades the prospect that your solution has the ability deliver what he or she needs, better than he or she can. The proposal should also provide justification, timelines, and investment figures for the entire portion of the prospect's commitment during the duration intended and in terms that are useful and understandable to the client.

Responses to RFPs require both adherence to the guidelines and requirements of the RFP, and a complete explanation of why and how the customer will benefit by awarding the contract to the selling company.

Qualified Prospect. In the sales process, a qualified prospect is a potential buyer that shows interest, has the budget and authority to buy, the desire to move forward in the sales process, and time available to implement the solution. A qualified prospect is different than a sales lead because a lead is just a name or someone who appears to be in the target market for the solution. A qualified prospect fits the same criteria as a sales lead, but then is "qualified" as someone who has

- the time to implement the solution
- the budget to make the purchase
- the need that can be solved by the solution
- the desire to continue in the sales process
- the decision-making authority to approve the purchase
- the ability to help facilitate a sale in the organization.

Revenue. In business, revenue is the amount of money that a company actually receives from its activities, mostly from sales of products and/or services to customers. To investors, revenue is less important than *profit*, or *income*, which is the amount of money the business has earned after deducting all business expenses. However, in sales, your quota and commissions are usually determined based on revenue you bring in.

Sales Cycle. A sales cycle is a length of time to initiate and complete a sale—to identify and qualify prospects, define the goods or services, and accept and acknowledge the order. The length of the sales cycle often depends on product complexity and degree of custom engineering, and may include the use of firm planned orders based on partially completed bills of material to order long lead time items. Some sales cycles take 30 days; some take six months to a year.

Sales Funnel. The sales funnel is a tool for the management of the sales process. Most salespeople use it to understand the sales pipeline and its status. The funnel is large at the top (representing prospects) and narrows at the bottom (representing closed sales). Remember, the traditional funnel is not the best tool for managing the entire experience of the customer, but it can help you identify areas for improvement and understand what actions can help the sales and marketing process to both increase deal flow and lower the cost of sales.

Sales Lead (aka suspect). A sales lead is usually the name of the first stage of a sales process. A "lead" is a person or group of persons identified as expressing some type of interest in a product or service. The lead may have a corporation or business associated with the person(s).

Sales leads come from either marketing lead-generation processes such as tradeshows, direct marketing, literature, and so on, or come from salesperson prospecting activities. For sales leads to convert to a prospect (or equivalently to move a lead from the process step sales lead to the process sales prospect), "qualification" must be performed and evaluated. Typically this involves identifying by direct questioning of the lead's product applicability, availability of funding, and timeframe for purchase. This is also the entry point of a sales funnel.

Once a lead exists in this stage, additional operations may be performed such as background research on the lead's employer, the general market that the lead belongs to, contact information beyond that provided initially, or other information useful for contacting and evaluating a lead for elevation to prospect—the next sales step.

Sales Presentation (aka sales pitch, sales script). How the product or service is described and promoted to the customer. The sales presentation is what the salesperson uses to attract attention and interest in verbal and written introductions to prospects—it has to be concise, yet thorough. The message in the sales presentation should also be used by the selling company in its various advertising and promotional material aimed at the target market. Traditionally, the selling company's marketing department would formulate the sales presentation, but these days salespeople greatly improve their selling effectiveness if they are able to refine and adapt the product offer (not the specification) for targeted sectors and individual major prospects.

Developing and tailoring a product offer, or proposition, is a vital part of the selling process, and the approach to this has changed over the years.

Sales Process. A sales process is a systematic methodology for performing product or service sales. The reasons for having a sales process include seller and buyer risk management, achieving standardized customer interaction in sales, and scalable revenue generation. Specific steps in sales processes vary from company to company but generally include the following:

1. Prospecting
2. Approaching
3. Qualifying
4. Presenting
5. Discovering
6. Committing
7. Following up

From a seller's point of view, a sales process mediates risk by providing milestones for deals based on a collection of information or execution of procedures that rate movement to the next step. This controls seller resource expenditure on nonperforming deals. Ideally this also prevents buyers from purchasing products they don't need, though such a benefit requires ethical intentions by the seller. Because of the uncertainty of this assurance, buyers often have a buying or purchasing process.

Sales processes are generally more common for companies that either have large revenue risks that require systematic assurance of revenue generation and/or those that choose to use a more consultative sales approach (such as Saturn, IBM, or Hewlett-Packard).

Strictly speaking, even an effective ad hoc or retail sales process can be described by steps of an ideal sales process, though some of the steps may be executed quickly. Often a bad sales experience can be analyzed and shown to have skipped key steps. This is where good sales processes mediate risk for both buyer and seller.

Many companies develop their own sales process. However, off-the-shelf versions are available from companies such as Huthwaite International and Miller Heiman. These companies provide a customizable process and a set of electronic tools that can be freestanding or integrated if required with the company's CRM or opportunity management system.

Terms and Conditions (aka Ts & Cs). For a legal contract, this will clearly create legally binding terms and conditions for the transaction. The terms and conditions spell out the rights and privileges of both the buyer and the seller, and what actions each may or must take. Examples include interest rate, length of payment terms, out-clauses, warranty, resell, copyrights, deferment options, late payment charges, and delinquency or default consequences, and so on.

Territory. A territory is a defined area usually considered to be the "possession" of the salesperson and/or selling organization. A territory is a geographic area in which a salesperson sells, and is established based on the selling strategy of the selling firm. It can be city specific or regionally specific. A territory is different from a vertical market focus (focused on industry, not necessarily on territory).

Transaction. The transaction is the hub of global commerce. A deal transaction is a unique event where money exchanges hands in return for a product or service. The "transaction experience" is the buying, selling, and marketing cycle defined as the pre- and post-effects of that unique sale.

The transaction itself holds a key position as the hub of commerce. Each sale is identified and handled separately as a unique transaction experience. Each time a signature is provided by the buyer, and a sale is consummated by the buying organization, a single transaction has occurred, but the transaction experience may only be halfway over.

Transaction Experience. The pre- and post-experience of the buying and selling organization surrounding a unique transaction. A transaction is one point in time where money changes hands. A transaction experience encompasses the marketing, selling, and fulfillment (customer service) experience.

Unique Selling Proposition (USP). A unique selling proposition is the strongest and most unique benefit for a given target market—*unique* being the operative word. Real or perceived uniqueness about your company is the most important aspect of the USP in the eyes of the buyer. Unique is also important because it generally causes a prospect to buy from one salesperson or supplier as opposed to another. USPs help a company sell the best against perceived competitors who don't have a strong USP.

Up-Sell. The sale of a product or service in addition to the product or service the customer has already purchased. For example, an agent may sell an additional feature such as voicemail with a new telephone service. You can only up-sell to existing customers. This is almost the same as cross-sell; it's just delineating the fact that the additional sale to an existing customer was for *the same line of product* purchased, not a different line.

Value Proposition (aka value prop). The value proposition should answer the consumer's most important question: "What's in it for me?" It is a clear and specific statement about the *tangible benefits* a consumer receives by using a product or service. A value proposition is a statement summarizing the customer targets, competitor targets, and the core strategy for how one intends to differentiate one's product from the offerings of competitors.

Vertical Market. A market that is narrow and deep; that is, it is limited to customers in a few industries and many producers in the industry use the product. It defines a group of businesses, organizations, or enterprises that are viewed on the basis of the unique and specific nature of the products or services that they sell (or buy) in the activities in which they are engaged.

APPENDIX E

Answers to Ethics Case Studies

In Step 7, I outline two ethical case studies for your consideration.

Ethics Case 1: The best possible answer is:

3. Do the best she can on the proposal and submit it without the information she doesn't have, on time.

Ethics Case 2: The best possible answer is:

2. Say nothing to John about what he knows and shift the conversation.

REFERENCES

Battell, C. 2006. *Effective Listening. Topline: How To Drive Sales.* Alexandria, VA: ASTD Press.

HR Chally. 2006. *What Makes an Excellent Sales Force.* Retrieved September 12, 2008, from http://www.esresearch.com/e/home/document.php?dA=Chally_1_Comp

Hickman, Stewart. 2009. *Hiring and Retaining Top-Performing Sales Performers. Topline: How To Drive Sales.* Alexandria, VA: ASTD Press.

Johansson, Frans. 2004. *The Medici Effect: Breakthrough Insights at the Intersection of Ideas, Concepts, and Cultures.* Boston, MA: Harvard Business School Press.

Lambert, Brian, Tim Ohai, and Eric Kerkhoff. 2009. *World-Class Selling: New Sales Competencies.* Alexandria, VA: ASTD Press.

Meginson, Leon C., Donald C. Mosley, and Paul H. Pietrie, Jr. 1986. *Management Concepts and Applications,* 2d ed. New York: Harper and Row Publishers, pp. 16–17.

Mikula, Jim. 2003. *Sales Training.* Alexandria, VA: ASTD Press.

Pelham, A. 2002. A Model and Test of the Influence of Firm Level Consulting-Oriented Sales Force Programs on Sales Force Performance. *Journal of Personal Selling & Sales Management.* Armonk, NY: M.E. Sharpe.

Rackham, Neil. 1988. *SPIN Selling.* New York: McGraw-Hill.

Steil, Lyman K., and Richard K. Bommelje. 2004. *Listening Leaders: The Ten Golden Rules to Listen, Lead & Succeed.* Edina, MN: Beaver's Pond Press, Incorporated.

Stevens, H., and T. Kinni. 2007. *Achieve Sales Excellence: The 7 Customer Rules for Becoming the New Sales Professional.* Avon, MA: Platinum Press.

INDEX

C

D

ABOUT THE AUTHOR

Brian Lambert is the director of Sales Training Drivers for the American Society for Training and Development (ASTD). He leads the sales profession-wide global competency modeling effort and research agenda to define what world-class salespeople and sales managers need to know and do to be successful.

Brian has 15 years of experience in all facets of sales, sales management, and sales training, and is an internationally recognized expert on transforming sales team systems, processes, and people through learning. His work has taken him to Europe, Africa, and North and South America, where he has personally trained over 15,000 salespeople and sales managers from across the globe. He has authored two other books on professional selling, including *World-Class Selling: New Sales Competencies*, published by ASTD Press. He has received winner's circle awards for sales performance and Air Force medals for leadership. In 2006, Brian was recognized by *Sales & Marketing Management* magazine as one of the most influential people in professional selling.

Brian has a master's of science degree in human resource and information resource management from Central Michigan University and a PhD in management from Capella University.